Drawing to Learn

Second Edition

Margaret Brooks

Published by Margaret Brooks

Design by BookCreate
BookCreate.com

ISBN 978-0-6454044-7-0

Printed in USA

Drawing to Learn

Second Edition

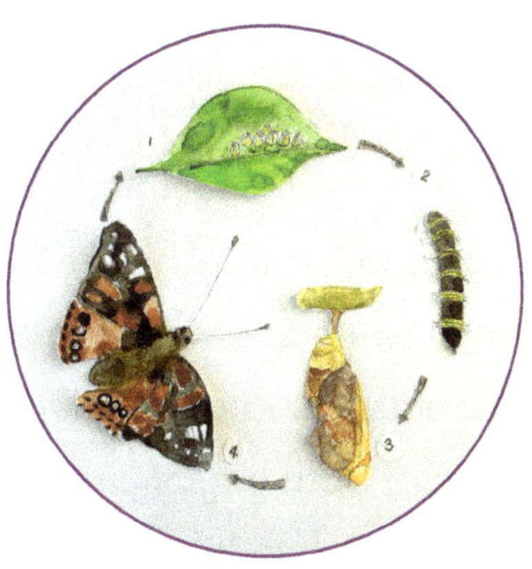

Margaret Brooks

About the Author

Dr Margaret Brooks is an adjunct Associate Professor at the University of New England, Australia. She has been researching drawing and art for almost thirty years. Her research focuses on young children's drawing processes and the relationship between drawing and meaning making from socio/cultural perspectives. She uses arts based and visual ethnographic methods to examine the drawing processes of both adults and young children. She is also a practicing artist. Her most recent artwork involves collaboration with artists, young children and art museums around environmental, cultural and social issues. Her studio work focuses on drawing and installation. She believes in the power of art to facilitate 'trans- actions' between people issues and places.

Margaret has a strong global audience and is the owner and editor of 'The 'International Art in Early Childhood' web site, and the editor for the 'International Art in Early Childhood Research Journal'.

See HTTPS://artinearlychildhood.org/

About this Book

Drawing and art making are core to programming in early childhood. We know that children use the arts to make sense of their world. But do we know how this happens and how best we can support it? Art is a form of communication, a language. For young children who do not yet read and write it is a primary means of communication.

But can we speak this language? Do we fully understand how the arts supports thinking and meaning making for young children? Much of early childhood practice rests on socio, cultural, historical theories. However, until now there has been no framework for the arts in early childhood that is congruent with these contemporary theories.

This book effectively addresses this gap in the literature. It is a scholarly work that carefully unpacks the art making processes of young children from a Vygotskian perspective. It illustrates and demonstrates through stories and samples of children's art making processes, how drawing and the arts are a leading activity in the development of the child. It links theory to practice to empower educators to support the artistic development of young children. It demonstrates how art studio practices, when braided with socio, cultural, historical theories provide a powerful tool for learning.

Table of contents

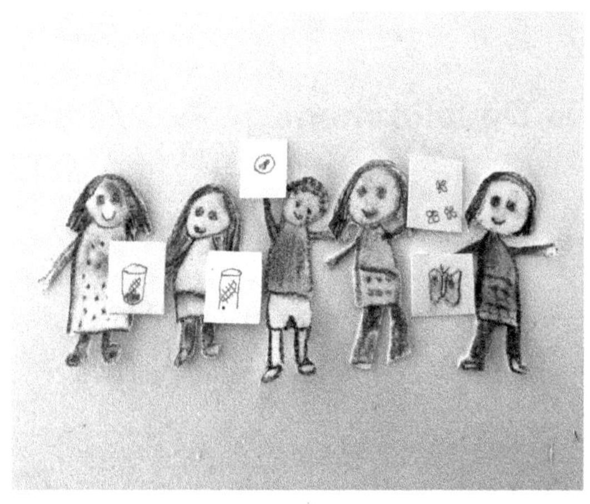

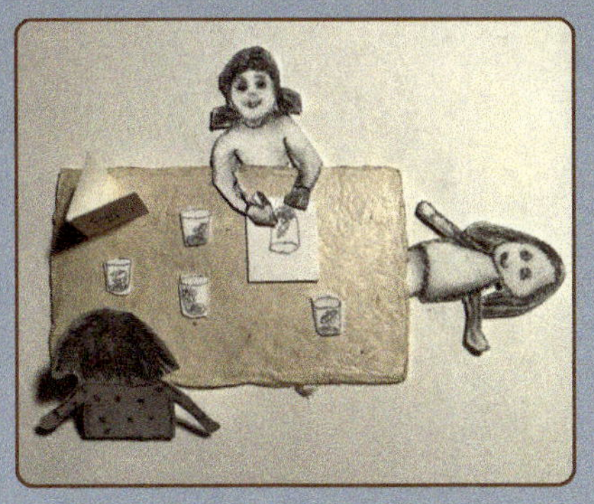

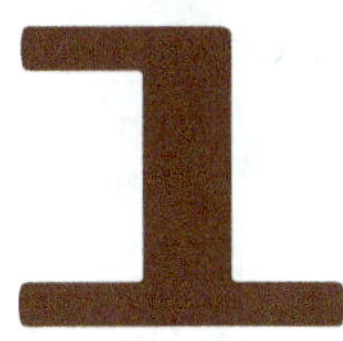

Why do children make art?

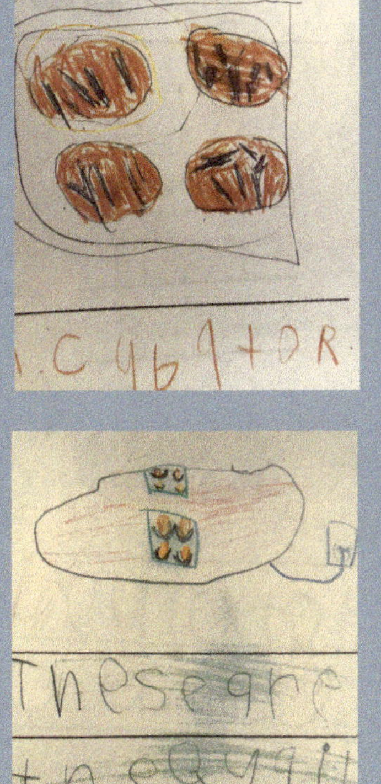

I had just introduced an incubator and six fertile eggs as part of our study of eggs. As I often did, I had laid out clipboards and pencils and was encouraging the children in my kindergarten class to make drawings. Several children made quick drawings of the insulated box, the window on top and eggs inside. As this experience was scientific in nature I encouraged them to label their drawings.

I noticed Joan had been sitting drawing near the incubator with great concentration. Unlike the others, she had not been doing an observation drawing, instead she had drawn an egg with a beautifully detailed embryo inside. I was both amazed and surprised. Amazed at the empathy of her drawing and surprised at her perspective and the huge amount of information that was contained within the drawing. She told me she had seen pictures in a book of what was inside an egg, and she was thinking that the eggs in the incubator might also look like this. I asked her what words we could put on her drawing to label the head, the feet, and so on. She looked at me in a surprised and hurt way. "But I've drawn all there is," she said.

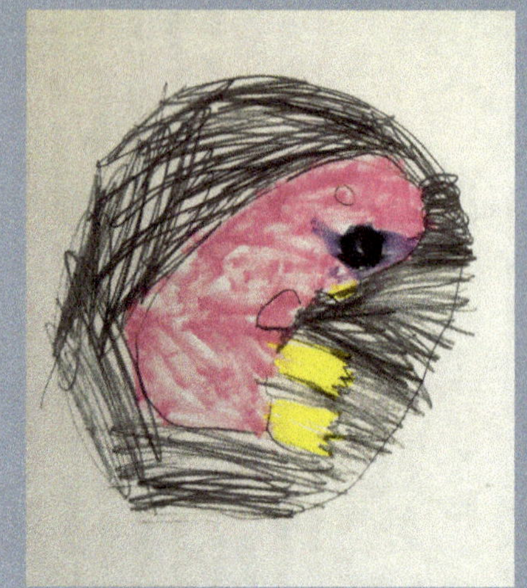

As teachers we give ourselves the role of art critic. We decide which work will be displayed and for what reason. We discuss our interpretations of children's drawings with colleagues. We define what is of value and what is not, what is good and what not so good. We become experts at reading children's drawings for developmental milestones, yet we seldom look at the context. We rarely invite the child to discuss her art with us or with others. In my approach to Joan's drawing, my teaching needs and assumptions took precedence over Joan's intentions for her drawing. I wanted to link her drawing with writing and use her work as a model for others in the class. Without entering into a dialogue that listened to Joan, I had imposed my own agenda.

Reflecting on this story, which I had captured in the reflective journal I kept at the time, I recall the words of Loris Malaguzzi of the Reggio Emilia schools in Italy. He reminds us that the spoken and written language are "increasingly imposed on children through imitative mechanisms which are poor in, or devoid of, interchange" (cited in the catalogue for the exhibition, Hundred languages of children, p23). It was Malaguzzi's words and the accompanying exhibition that prompted my search for a deeper understanding of young children's art making and our roles as teacher.

Art as Language

For young children, art is an important form of communication, one of the many languages they use to speak. For those who are not yet able to read and write, it is one of their primary modes of communication.

Children make art to express personal perceptions, thoughts, and feelings. Their artwork is a representation of the world as seen through their eyes. This process of representation helps them make sense of what they see and experience. Our understanding of children's representations draws us closer to their vision of the world. Many early childhood educators value children's artwork for the insights it gives into children's thinking.

Art making encompasses a very wide range of media. However, foundational to the visual arts is drawing, and it is on drawing that I will focus. Drawing is something children do most days, and we are all familiar with it. Drawing is an important part of many aspects of our lives and not just

Drawing by a four year old about learning to play and make friends

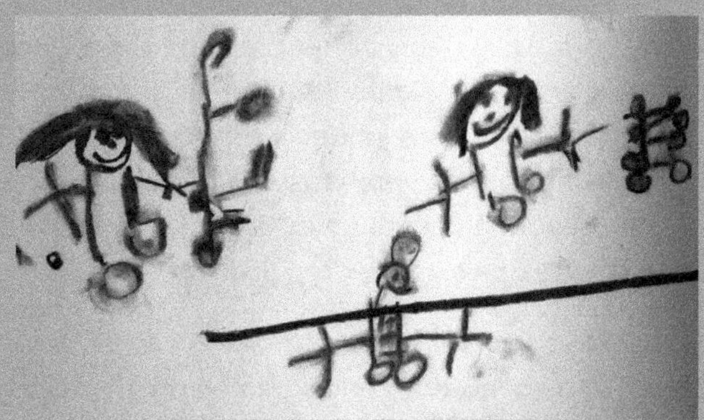

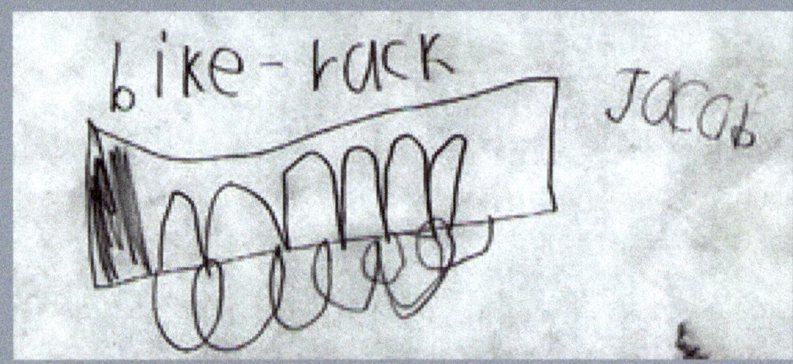

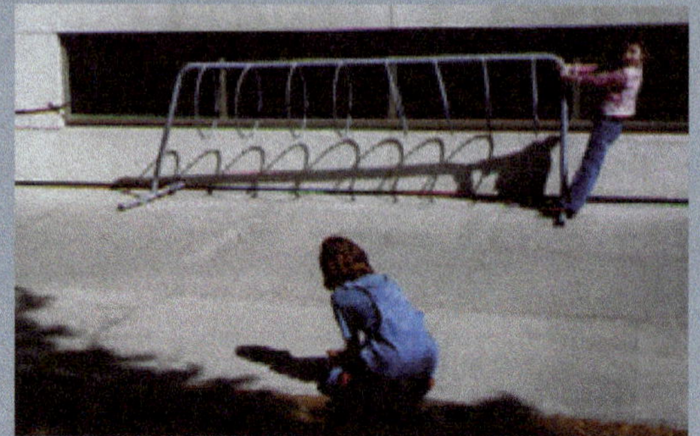

Why are shadows not the same as the object making the shadow?

something artists do. Drawing is connected to thinking and an important tool for sharing ideas, problem solving, and creating.

Art is always about something. Children often draw in an effort to make sense of their world. In order to support this meaning-making process, we need to discover the big ideas and the intentions behind the children's art-making efforts. As educators, we also need to learn for ourselves the kind of graphic problems children encounter and to have a large repertoire of strategies we can share with them. We need to know the possibilities afforded by different media. We can then share these with children so that they might expand their art making repertoires.

Unpacking children's art-making processes is challenging. Art-making events are complex and multilayered. Each child brings all of his or her previous experiences to the art making. Each child has a different set of skills and each a different intent. Art making for children does not necessarily have the same intent as artists who are influenced by the agendas of galleries, art movements, and the politics of art. Art making for children has more to do with everyday life and phenomena they encounter. While the art of young children has certain aesthetic qualities adults name and pursue, these are rarely the children's goals.

How can we best support young children's art making efforts? There is no simple recipe I can share. But I can introduce you to a sound theoretical framework that will guide you; a framework that is compatible with current practices in early childhood.

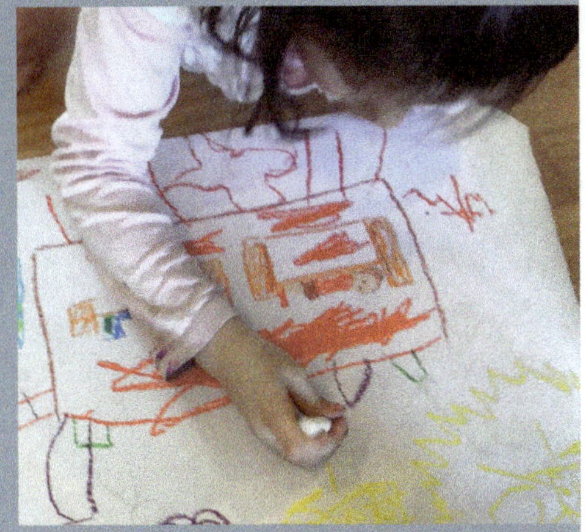

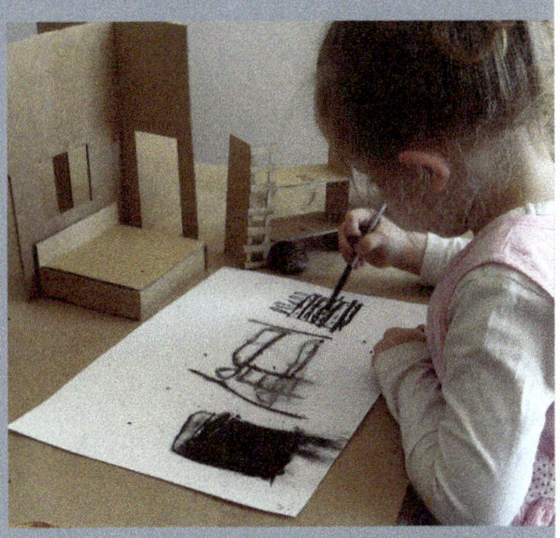

Bringing home knowledge into preschool through their drawings

In this book I unpack children's art making processes from a Vygotskian perspective to better understand how young children use the visual arts to make sense of their world and how we can best support them with their art and meaning making. Vygotsky saw new knowledge and ideas emerging from the social environment where children are supported by more competent others. This view frees children from the constraints of fixed age/stage theories and opens up possibilities for growth and development. Adults have an active role in mediating meaning and sharing aspects of the culture. I will explore the many interesting roles an adult can take.

I take a closer look at the relationship between thought and art making, specifically drawing. I will explore the meaning making capacities of the visual arts in relation to learning. Vygotsky suggests that we need language in order to think and make meaning. When we have names or labels for things, we are able to put ideas out there for examination. Otherwise, thoughts are confined to the individual's head. While Vygotsky focused mainly on speech, he also listed drawing as a meaning-making language. Children's art making is a cognitive process that leads their learning and is integral to their ongoing development. When art is used by the children within the social groupings of their peers in the classroom, it is part of a wider system of representation that includes talking, gestures, facial expressions, writing, model making, and role play. The relationship between art and the context in which it is being used is of primary importance. We need to have a clear and deep understanding of how the child is using art/drawing to make sense of the world in which they live and the important role of the adult to support those efforts.

Reading Young Children's Representations

Here are two small examples that highlight some of the difficulties children encounter while drawing and might prompt you to think more deeply about children's representations: the intent behind the art work, the big ideas children pursue through art, how we can respond to their art making, and what we can learn from their art.

The tadpoles' eyes

It was spring and the children had brought some tadpoles to preschool to study. The teacher put them in a large trough on a tabletop along with some pondweed and gravel from the pond. Around the trough she put some clipboards, paper, graphite pencils and watercolor pencils. Each day small groups of children would record what the tadpoles were doing and how they were growing. Here is what two of the children drew one day when they discovered that tadpoles had eyes.

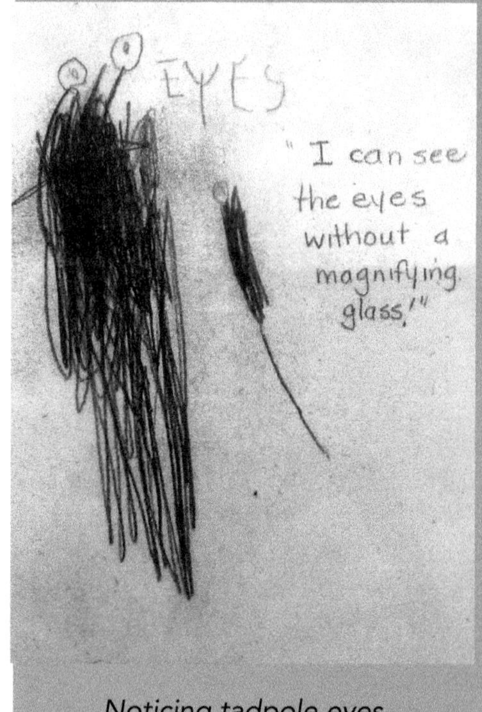

Noticing tadpole eyes

As an educator, how might you respond to this drawing? If your own self-efficacy in the arts was low, or if you did not have a theoretical framework that made sense to you, you might just say, "nice drawing" or "well done," and pass on by. Or, if you believed that art development is a sequence of naturally occurring stages where drawing progresses from scribbles to realism, you might think that this child was still at a very beginning stage and does not yet know where a tadpole's eyes are. You might also not discuss the drawing of the eyes with the child because you believe that we should not interfere with children's art making. Each of these responses leaves the child without any support for drawing. When these responses are what usually happens, then not only is the child is unable to progress but she might also believe that her drawing is of no value and give up the struggle to draw. If the teacher had the same lack of an adequate response for writing, then her role as a competent educator would be in question. Unfortunately, there are too many educators who cannot adequately support the arts.

However, this child's teacher had been actively watching and now engaged the child in conversation about what she had been doing. The child explained that when she colored the head very black as she saw it, the graphite would then not allow her to draw anything on top of the heavy dark bits. But she wanted to record the eyes so she chose to draw them off to one side. She told her teacher that she knew where the eyes were and it was just because she could not get them to show up on the black that she chose to put them somewhere else. She was happy with her solution because she could now see how both the head and the eyes looked.

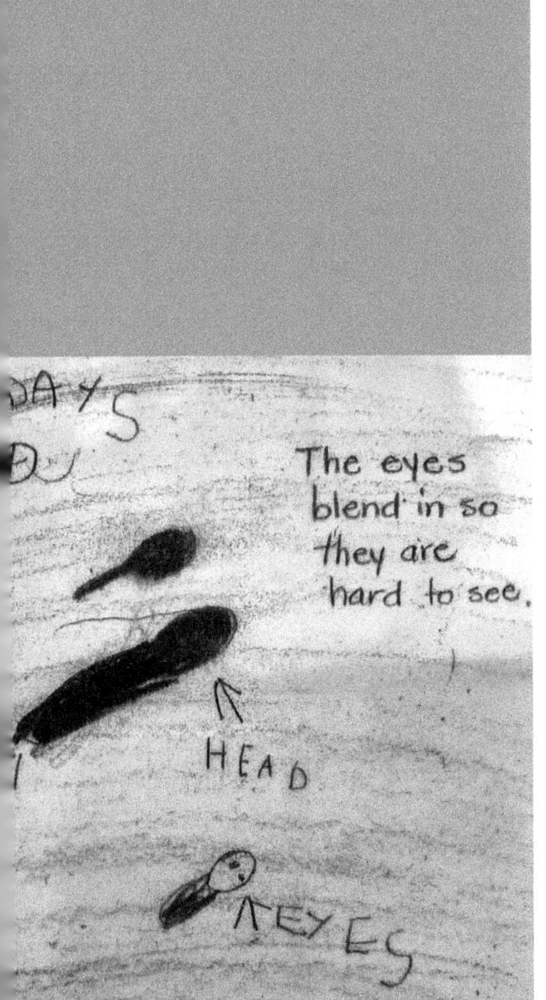

Solutions for drawing eyes

Her friend next to her had a similar problem, but she had a different solution. She drew three tadpoles, two colored in to show the dark head and the other uncolored to show the eyes.

This teacher's practice was guided by her deep understanding of the importance of talking with children about their drawings and trying to find out what their big ideas were and what their intent was. She was keen to know what the children were thinking as they were drawing and often sat and talked and drew next to them.

In this instance the children were struggling with the drawing medium. They did not yet know that you cannot easily draw on top of graphite. They knew how to draw but the medium was not co-operating. This event clearly demonstrated that we cannot analyze children's drawings out of context, nor can we make assumptions about what is happening without talking to the child.

Planting potatoes

A few weeks later the same class decided to plant some potatoes. The teacher asked the children to draw what they thought might happen when they planted potatoes. Here is one child's drawing.

Life cycle of a potato

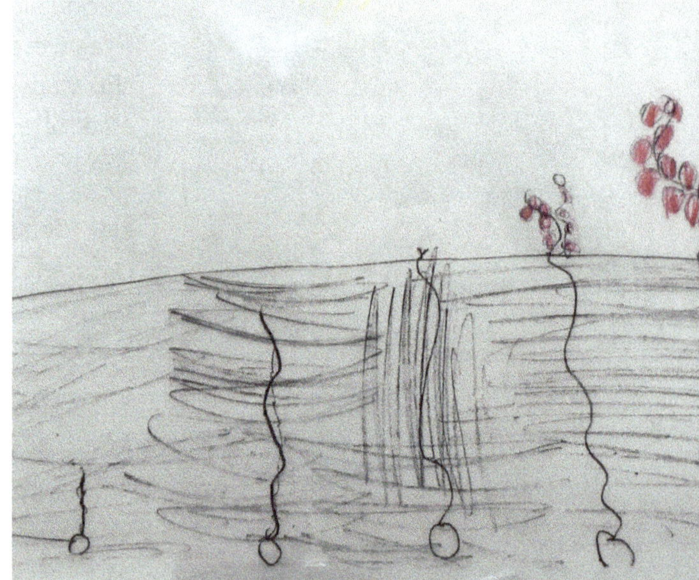

She has shown the various stages of growth of the potato and that the plant needs sun and rain. When the teacher first looked at the drawing she assumed the plant had red leaves. However, the child was quick to correct her and let her know that the red circles were the potatoes growing and almost ready to be picked.

Here is an example of a drawing reflecting the child's socio-cultural background and home knowledges. She had experienced picking tomatoes in the family garden but had never planted or picked potatoes. She generalized her knowledge about harvesting tomato plants to the potatoes.

If we as teachers only have our current age/stage developmental categories to guide our understanding of children's art, we might be tempted to undervalue these drawings. We might classify them as lacking and assess the child as not yet performing at the appropriate level. These two events demonstrate that children often use the arts as a tool for learning. However, our current beliefs and practices do not adequately support children's efforts in the arts. I believe what is missing in the arts is a strong social constructionist framework, that is compatible with our other early childhood frameworks, to guide our programming and practice in the arts. Vygotsky suggests that learning leads development. Therefor there is a strong role for a more competent other to provide support to move children's art learning forward.

The State of Art Education

All is not well in the teaching of art in early childhood. There is a mismatch of theoretical frameworks between the visual arts in early childhood and early childhood generally. While most of early childhood as a discipline has moved to embrace contemporary social constructionist theories, teaching the arts in early childhood still relies on outdated developmental theories. Early childhood educators are still holding on to the teachings of child psychologist Jean Piaget and art professor Victor Lowenfeld. While I recognize that we don't want to discard everything from the past, there are beliefs and practices from their teachings that run counter to current theories. Piaget and Lowenfeld saw the artistic development of young children unfolding naturally in an individualistic, developmental sequence. They believed that ability in the arts was an innate gift that we had little influence over. Such beliefs indicate a hands-off interpretation for teaching art that requires the teacher to stand back and not interfere with the natural order of development. This is not a response compatible with current practice in other domains.

The other dominant framework for the arts is the discipline-based perspective from the Modernist era. It involves viewing and analyzing the elements of art where, for example, paintings are analyzed according to qualities of shape, line, and tone. Discipline-based design elements were developed as a tool for viewing the more traditional drawings, paintings, and prints of the modernist era and previous era art. However, they do not work so well for viewing contemporary art.

You can imagine that if we were to apply these criteria to the tadpole drawings teachers would completely miss the point and again undervalue the work of the child. Such traditional perspectives do not address how we might respond to postmodern art or to contemporary art like installation, video, ephemeral, and performance art. A discipline-based perspective also does not acknowledge the intent of the child, nor does it support the child's exploration of meaning through the arts. Yet this is still the dominant discourse for art in early childhood. Not only does it not fit the art of this century but such a discourse is not congruent with the socio-cultural theories of early childhood today. Postmodern art more closely aligns with the sociocultural theories of early childhood. It challenges the traditional boundaries and definitions of art, rejecting the notion of a singular narrative or objective truth. Postmodern visual art often engages in self-reflexivity, deconstruction, and a playful juxtaposition of images and ideas. It explores the intersections of different artistic mediums, blurring the lines between painting, sculpture, photography, and installation. Artists working within the postmodern framework frequently critique established norms, conventions, and power structures, while embracing the idea of multiple perspectives and subjective interpretations. This results in a vibrant and dynamic art form that encourages viewers to question preconceived notions, engage in critical thinking, and actively participate in the construction of meaning.

It must be confusing for children to be presented with models that do not reflect their everyday experiences of life and of contemporary art. Young children find the elements of design too abstract to be helpful in their art making.

Such frameworks and beliefs, that result in a hands-off approach to the arts with young children, are not compatible with current socio-cultural practices like intentional teaching and active pedagogy. More worrying, the artistic outcome for the child that results from this lack of engagement and lack of adult or expert guidance is the well-documented decline in artistic efficacy about age eight when many children give up the arts, believing they do not have the capacity for it (Davis 1997).

Teacher training

Recent research (Denee 2022, Lindsay 2017) has uncovered a widespread lack of self-efficacy in the visual arts among early childhood educators. Many believe they have nothing to offer young children, so they do not engage with this component of programming. These early childhood teachers do not feel competent or comfortable teaching art. They do not draw and are not happy with the results if they do. They do not see themselves as being competent to model drawing or teach art. Children are aware of such insecurity in their teachers and are often influenced to also feel insecure. Teachers rightly point out that they have never been taught to draw. Visual art has not been a part of their studies. The arts have been squeezed out of preservice early childhood teacher training. We know that unless we have firsthand experience of something, it is often difficult to fully appreciate the complexity and nuances of the task. Like learning to write or swim, it is hard to understand the problems involved if we have never experienced them. Educators need to have a repertoire of visual arts skills so they can support children's art making practices. Trying on "being artist" is an important component of teacher training. It will give us first-hand experiences of the many challenges artists and children have to surmount.

The aim of this text is to demonstrate what a social constructionist theory might look like for the visual arts, and in particular drawing. I am going to take some key ideas of Lev Vygotsky, the father of social constructionism, and his followers and apply them to the visual arts. When art, like play, is one of the activities that is leading learning, we need to come to a deeper understanding of how we can support children's use of this essential tool. When children are not yet able to read and write, the visual arts are their primary mode of communication. This text presents a strong, contemporary theoretical framework for the visual arts, one that is congruent with other curriculum areas, so that the arts can become central to programming and planning for young children.

Before we look forward, I believe it is helpful to take a quick look back and contextualise the framework I want to present.

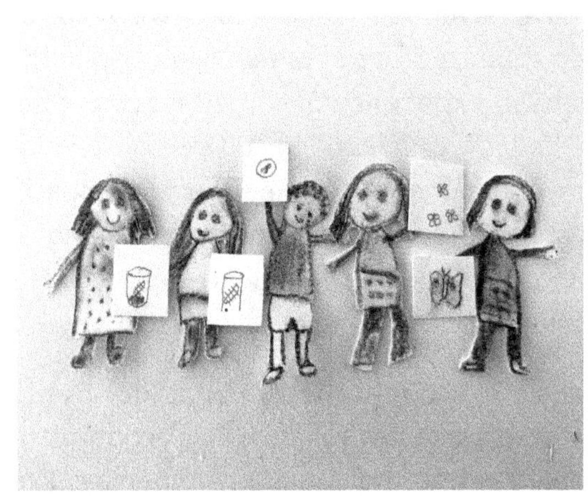

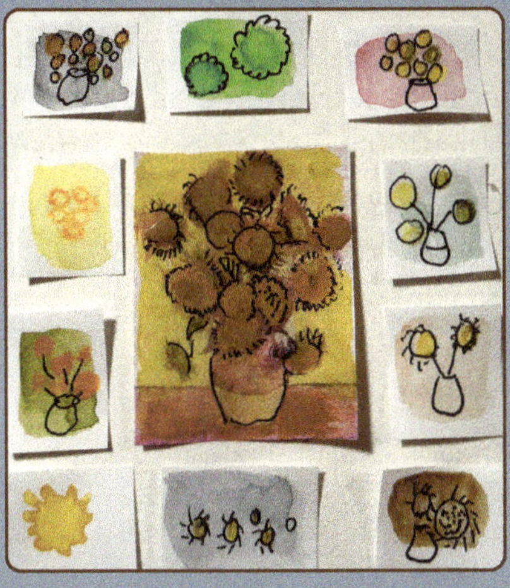

2

Looking Back and Looking Forward

A historical look at some of the better known theories and studies in art education will provide us with an understanding of how we arrived where we are. It will also illuminate ideas and practices that are still prevalent and perhaps need both a closer look and more critical consideration. Hopefully it will demonstrate that while much work has been done there is still much more to do. It will help us see the gaps in our knowledge and the possibilities for future research.

A drawing lesson from late 1800's. Copying the teacher

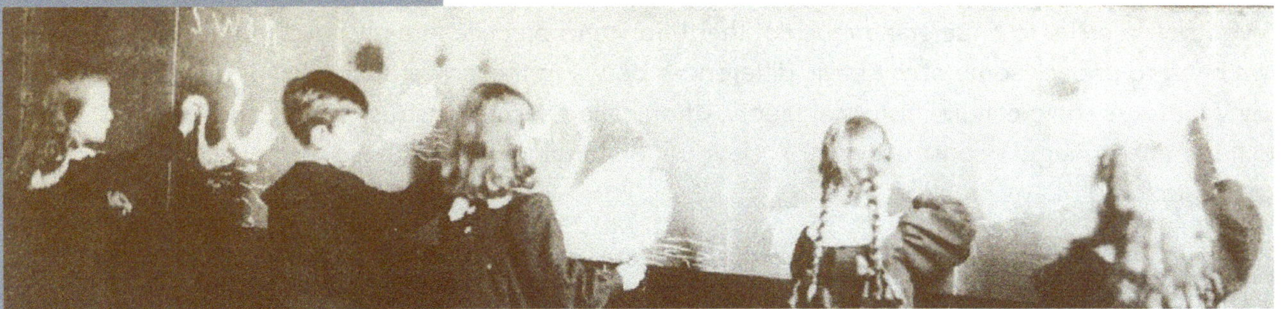

One of the problems we encounter when we look at the art of young children is the use of the word art. Art means many things to many people (Kindler 1997, 82). Art is redefined over time as different art movements take place. Art is reflective of the social and cultural context in which it occurs. Artists respond to events of their time and place. Different eras and different art movements and aesthetics will bring different theoretical perspectives to the question of what art is for (Wilson and Wilson 1982). Asking what art is for when we are considering young children making art is challenging. The answer depends upon which perspective we take and on which theoretical lens we are looking through. Different aesthetic and theoretical positions will lead to very different interpretations of children's art and very different provisions for and responses to children doing art.

We also have to consider the relationship between children's art and adult artists' art. Are there commonalities between the two or are they completely different? We don't often see children's art work in galleries nor do children usually work towards exhibitions, yet children's art holds great fascination for us and we enjoy its freshness and aesthetics.

Given the breadth of the topic art, I narrowed the focus on children's drawing. Drawing is foundational and underpins each aspect of the visual arts. I am not only interested in the finished art work but rather I want to understand how the drawing came into being and what the relationship is between the drawing, thinking, and meaning for the child.

Vygotsky and Piaget

Our understanding of how children learn hugely influences the way we teach. Theory and practice in early childhood education is underpinned by the work of two great thinkers, Jean Piaget and Lev Vygotsky. In order to understand much of the theory and practice in early childhood art education we need to unpack some of the basic differences between these two giants. What do we mean by Vygotsky's socio cultural historical theory, often called social constructionism, and how is it different from Piaget's constructivism? A clear understanding of both these terms is critical for our understanding of arts practices.

Knowing a little about Vygotsky's life helps us understand his work and put it in context. It is important to have a good understanding of his theories so that we can be truly reflective practitioners. Vygotsky was born in Russia in 1896 and died of tuberculosis at age thirty-seven. He was a prolific writer but his early death meant that some of his work was not fully developed. Vygotsky is considered the father of the social constructionist movement (that some refer to as sociocultural historical theory) that now underpins most early childhood programming and practice today.

Vygotsky was a contemporary of Piaget. Piaget was born in Switzerland in 1890 and lived until 1980. Piaget too was a prolific writer. He was considered the father of constructivism and was a well-established theorist in Western education. Vygotsky was familiar with Piaget's early writing and often critiqued Piaget's work. While the writings of Piaget were freely available around the globe from early in the century, the Cold War did not allow the writing of Vygotsky to reach the West until much later. It was not until the early 1970s that his writing was available globally. When western scholars first read them, they caused quite a controversy because many of the theories he proposed were so different from those of Piaget and in fact anything previously seen. Educators in the West had only just come to terms with Piaget and were slow to appreciate Vygotsky's work. Now, many of his ideas have been tried and tested and gained popularity. However, his concepts and theories are often difficult to understand and many educators only have a superficial knowledge of his work. Most people rely on others' interpretations of his theories. Nonetheless his theories resonated with many and have been a springboard for a growing body of writing that guides and influences our practices today. Vygotsky has brought us new ideas about the way children learn. It is worth the effort to read his theories. His two most popular books are *Thought and Language* and *Mind in Society*.

Social constructionism has its roots in Vygotsky's theories of teaching and learning. Vygotsky suggests that the learner brings prior knowledge that combines with new knowledge through their interaction with others. That is to say, knowledge is co-constructed. Past and present social interactions influence cognitive construction. Vygotsky believed that our life experiences affect and influence our development and learning. The social context influences learning and shapes how and what we think. From a Vygotskian perspective, everything about learning and development is social. Hence the name social constructionism. Vygotsky's developmental theory differs in significant ways from Piaget and other theories of child development.

For Piaget, intellectual development has a universal nature independent of the child's cultural context. He proposed distinct and sequential stages with children reaching the highest level, formal operational thinking, around age fourteen. However, for Vygotsky, the social and cultural context was of primary concern and it determined the type of cognitive processess that emerged. Piaget emphasized the child's interactions with physical objects in developing mature forms of thinking, while Vygotsky emphasized the child's interactions with people.

When we look closely at art education in early childhood today we find it is still heavily influenced by the developmental, cognitive constructivist theories of Piaget. Piaget, in turn, drew heavily on the developmental theories of George Henri Luquet (1927). Luquet used naturalistic observations to describe stage-like progressions in children's drawing. He assumed that children's drawings were based on an internal mental model.

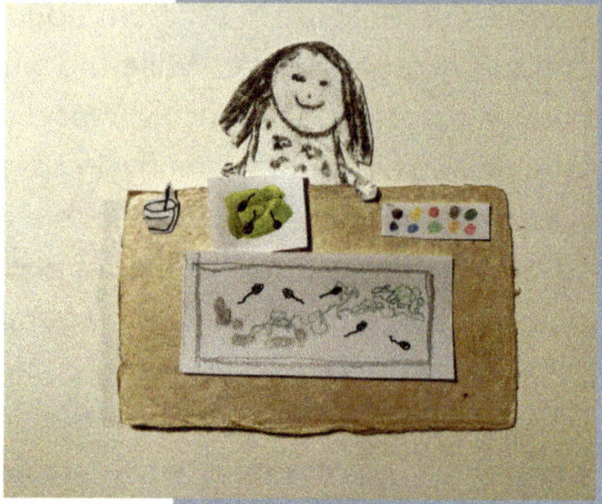

Luquet identified five stages of development. In the first stage, "fortuitous realism" a child recognizes a likeness between their spontaneous scribble and something known to them in the world. The child's discovery that their marks can be representational leads to more intentional mark making. Lauquet calls the next stage "failed realism" when referring to the child's inadequate skills for producing a likeness, and "synthetic incapacity" when referring to the child's inability to place marks in correct spatial relationships. The first stage of successful intentional representation is called "intellectual realism." This is where the child draws not only what they see but also what they know. The child then progressed onto the last stage, "visual realism." This is where there is a high degree of verisimilitude between the subject and the drawing.

Piaget adopted Luquet's ideas and incorporated them into his developmental framework (Piaget and Inhelder 1969). However, for Piaget, drawing was not a special domain of development but merely a window into the child's general cognitive progress. He argued that a child's drawing performance reflected the child's cognitive competence. This meant that until a child reached Piaget's concrete operational stage of development, they were tied to egocentric mental models of the world. For example, a child cannot combine concepts of perpendicularity, parallelism, seriation, and proportion until they enter fully into the stage of concrete operations. Only then, at this stage, can they produce visually realistic drawings.

Piaget's age/stage framework of cognitive development was, and still is, hugely influential in early childhood education and particularly in art education, resulting in a curriculum that reflects this framework. This curriculum is full of sequential activities that are tied to stage/age dependent behaviours. It builds on the assumption that children's growth is a naturally unfolding process that cannot essentially be changed (Freedman 1997, 95).

I find this table developed by Joan Wink and LeAnn Putney (2002) very useful. It clearly differentiates between cognitive constructivist and social constructionist points of view.

Construct	**Piaget** **Cognitive Constructivist**	**Vygotsky** **Social Constructionist**
Knowledge	Changing body of knowledge, individually constructed in social world.	Changing body of knowledge, mutually constructed with others.
Learning	• Active construction, restructuring prior knowledge. • Multiple opportunities and diverse processes to connect to what is already known. • Interaction with others and environment.	• Collaborative construction of socially/culturally defined knowledge and values. • Socially and culturally constructed opportunities, tying to students' experience. • Collaboration with others through social/cultural setting.

Construct	Piaget Cognitive Constructivist	Vygotsky Social Constructionist
Teaching	Challenge students' thinking towards more complete understanding (guide on the side).	• Co-construct knowledge with students by sharing expertise and understanding. • Actuator of learning.
Motivation	Self-development, competence.	Collective and individual development through collaboration.
Role of teacher	Facilitator, guide.	Mediator, mentor, actuator.
Actions	Create opportunities for interacting with meaningful ideas, materials, others.	Construct with students' opportunities for Interacting with meaningful ideas, materials, and others.
Role of student	Active construction within mind.	Active thinker, explainer, interpreter, inquirer, active social participator.
Student view of self	Sense-maker, problem solver.	Sense-maker, problem solver, socially appropriate member of collective.

Construct	Piaget Cognitive Constructivist	Vygotsky Social Constructionist
Role of peers	• Not necessarily encouraged, but can stimulate thinking, raise questions. • Process of inquiry.	Assume part of knowledge construction, contribute to definition of knowledge, help define opportunities for learning.
Evidence of learning	• Performance: explanation of reasoning. • Ongoing assessment.	• Process of inquiry, socially competent participation in the collective. • Performance: explanation of reasoning, social performance over multiple sites.
Purpose of school	Create new knowledge, learn strategies to continue learning.	Create new knowledge, learn strategies to continue learning. Prepare individuals as social members with expanding repertoires of appropriate ways of interacting.

Toward a More Social Constructionist Framework

I will now try to document some of the important shifts in thinking that show the gradual movement toward a more social constructionist framework for art in early childhood.

There were very few educators who challenged the notion that children's drawings ought to be allowed to mature naturally without any outside influences, by either imitation or instruction. Brent and Marjorie Wilson (1982) studied children's spontaneous drawings. They found that these children taught themselves to draw by copying from a whole range of other graphic images found in their culture. They contended that young children learned to draw mainly through imitation and influence. They proposed that children should indeed be encouraged to share their drawing skills with each other as well as copy the work of well-known artists in order to learn to draw better. This approach to drawing instruction draws upon traditional European art school practices of learning from the Masters, a sort of apprenticeship model. The Wilsons asserted that both the ease of acquisition of symbols and the flexible way that drawing allows ideas to be developed makes drawing an essential activity that should be encouraged in children.

The 1980s also saw a new approach to the art curriculum for grades K to 12. Introduced by the Getty Trust in the United States and called Discipline Based Art Education. DBAE was a good fit for the recommendations of the Wilsons. It emphasized four areas of study; aesthetics, art criticism, art history, and art production. Under the art production section there was a strong emphasis on learning skills and techniques. On the one hand, it advocated that art education was for all children, but on the other hand, the academic and standardized framework underpinning it was criticized as being too formulaic. It was not pluralistic enough. It called for a wider range of viewpoints. However, this curricular model remains strong and is still used today in K–12 programs.

At this time Elliott Eisner and Howard Gardner were influential voices in early childhood art education. Elliot Eisner listed seven myths that dominated art pedagogy. The most contentious myth was that children's art making should not be interfered with. General wisdom held that children should just be given lots of materials and freedom. Despite Eisner strongly opposing this myth, it seems to be still well embedded in early childhood practice. Other myths held by art educators were that art processes were more important than products and that children saw the world more clearly than adults. Eisner warned art educators and researchers to reexamine their beliefs and practices with all the clarity they could muster. Eisner was a powerful voice in art education and was instrumental in introducing alternative ways of looking at and responding to children's art. His book, The Arts and the Creation of Mind (2002), has been influential in promoting the arts in schools. In this book Eisner listed ten things he believed the arts gave children (Eisner 2002). The Arts:

- teach children to make good judgments about qualitative relationships
- teach children that problems can have more than one solution
- celebrate multiple perspectives
- teach children that in complex forms of problem solving purposes are seldom fixed, but change with circumstance and opportunity
- make vivid the fact that neither words in their literal form nor numbers exhaust what we can know
- teach students that small differences can have large effects
- teach students to think through and within a material
- help children learn to say what cannot be said
- enable us to have experience we can have from no other source and through such experience to discover the range and variety of what we are capable of feeling
- hold a position in the school curriculum that symbolizes to the young what adults believe is important

Howard Gardner, a contemporary of Eisner, is another strong advocate for the arts in early childhood. Gardner developed the theory of multiple intelligences. He refuted the idea that learning only took place through text-based instruction and evaluation. He found the idea that there could only be one single intelligence too restrictive and recognized that it did not account for other kinds of learning that were clearly observable. He laid out his theory of multiple intelligences in a book called Frames of Mind (Gardner 1983). Here he listed and discussed eight kinds of intelligence he had found.

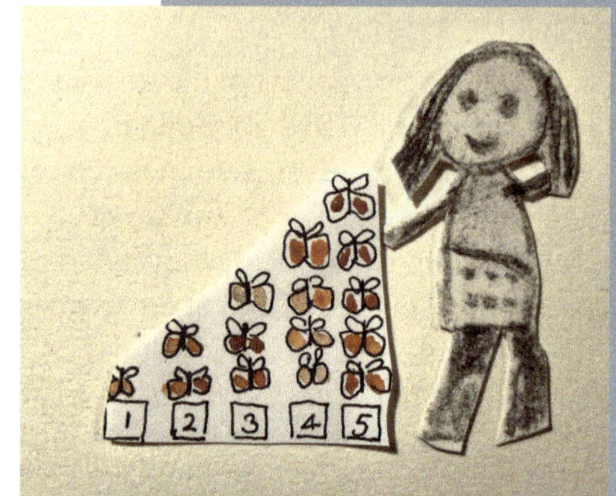

Gardner's work had a huge impact on education as a whole and in particular the arts. Not only did his theory validate teachers' own observations of children learning in many different ways, but it also gave them alternative ways of planning, programming, and teaching that would meet the diverse needs of children, often through the arts.

Gardner was senior director of Harvard's Project Zero for many years, which was founded in 1967. Its mission is to "understand and enhance learning, thinking and creativity for individuals and groups in the arts and other disciplines" (http://www.pz.harvard.edu/). Project Zero consists of a loosely knit group of researchers who are interested in understanding more about how the arts fit into education and how children learn in and through the arts. Over the past many years, the group has undertaken many research projects to look at the relationship between thinking and learning and consider how the arts contribute to the lives of children. It is worth visiting their extensive website. This group was among the first few to find more holistic ways of looking at and understanding art. They sometimes drew upon Vygotsky's conception of the nature of development and its relationship to culture.

Our understanding of culture is critical to our understanding of the development of children's aesthetic development (Newton and Kantner 1997). Just as the word art is complex and multi-faceted, so too is the word culture. In the 1980s, Vygotsky's socio-cultural theory was beginning to be seen as a valuable contribution to new ways of thinking about development. The importance of the role of a more competent other in helping to move development forward was gaining momentum. Thinking about artistic development that acknowledges the role of the social context was also beginning to gather interest (Bruner 1983, Cole, Gay, Glick, and Sharp 1971). Fresh definitions and ideas about culture add further support to current understanding of the intricate relationships between art and its cultural context.

In the 1990s, Anna Kindler and Bernard Darras approached the notion of plurality in drawing (Kindler and Darras 1997). That is, rather than thinking about artistic development as a linear progression, they developed the metaphor of a map. This model describes three segments of artistic development. The first segment deals with gestation, birth, and development of pictorial imagery in the early childhood years. The second segment is concerned with the phenomenon of initial imagery; a basic, stable, and efficient system of pictorial representation which seems commonly accessible, e.g when children draw recognizable objects, people and things they see. The third segment describes the many roads that may be followed in the development of pictorial imagery. These roads are not to be regarded as mutually exclusive choices, since one may travel through many of them throughout life (Darras 1997). They suggest that as children develop, they develop an expanding repertoire of strategies for pictorial representation that they apply according to the perceived needs and functions of their drawings and the context in which their work is produced. They note the differences between work that is created at home and school, spontaneous drawing, and drawing that is completed in response to a specific task. They argue for the necessity of an extended repertoire of what is understood to be drawing.

In my work with drawing and young children I too have noticed the expanding set of drawing repertoires that children acquire. They are quite diverse and are often learned on a need-to-know basis. Children I have worked with actively seek ideas, suggestions, and instructions for their drawing. How frustrating and confusing it must be when a teacher declines to help.

Which brings me to the most disturbing piece of research I have found on drawing. In 1997, Darras wrote about the U curve of graphic development. Initially, young children's art is seen as having the same aesthetic qualities as those of professional artists. However, between the age of five and eleven this artistic competency drops off and then plateaus, never to be regained. Traditionally this loss has been seen as something inevitable and irreversible unless the adolescent or adult decides to make art their chosen career and regain their competency. She challenges the education community's lack of concern for this loss of a meaning-making skill and advocates that drawing be taught every day just as math and writing are.

One of the characteristics of the postmodern world is the increased interest in pursuing multiple interpretations and meanings. However, when we are considering drawing, we find that many believe the goal of drawing is to produce a high level of verisimilitude between the subject and the drawing. This is an unacceptable expectation. Drawing is a responsive activity. In responsive drawing, comprehending the reality of a subject precedes and affects the qualities of our responses. When we draw, we are making intuitive choices and judgements that are driven by our perception, our experiences, our memories, and our observations. My drawing is a reflection of, and response to, what I see, know, and understand.

When we look at children's acquisition of a meaningful graphic language, we have to be careful that we are not looking for faithful replicas of the subject. We have to be open to the many interpretations and responses to the subject. We have to appreciate the competency of young children to respond and represent, to deal successfully with the duality of the object in the real world and its graphic representation. I believe that the children's ability to differentiate between the object and its representation allowed the children in my studies to use graphic images to pursue ideas and questions they had about the world in which they lived. When children draw their ideas, plans, and problems, we are able to literally see what they mean and are better able to talk with them and assist them.

Research in the arts is beginning to acknowledge the importance of the social and cultural contexts in which drawing occurs as well as the processes involved in drawing. There are calls for new ways of looking at the development of drawing, one that is more cognisant of the many-voiced nature of drawing. There is still much work to be done in this area, and many have called for more interdisciplinary collaboration and discussion among psychologists, art theorists, artists, and educators.

Visual Art and Education in the Twenty-First Century.

No review of the arts in early childhood would be complete without looking at the teaching in the Reggio Emilia preschools and infant toddler centers in northern Italy. Established after the second World War, these schools have such faith in the arts that each children's center has an atelier and resident atelierista. The atelier is a dedicated creative studio for young children where learning through the arts is given priority. The children's artistic and creative thinking is supported by the atelierista. The practice, philosophies, writings, and research that has emerged from these centers are at the forefront of early childhood education globally. Two important and popular books come from there; Carolyn Edwards, Lella Gandini and George Forman's book The Hundred Languages of Children: The Reggio Emilia Experience in Transformation was one of the first books to document the work of these preschools and remains a popular text today. It discusses key ideas such as constructing an understanding of children as important community members, the hundred languages of learning, teaching through relationships, and pedagogical documentation. Vea Vechi's book, Art and creativity in Reggio Emilia: Exploring the role and potential of ateliers in early childhood education, discusses some key ideas about the arts and creativity in the Reggio centers. Vea was an atelierista in a Reggio Emilia center.

In this century there has been great interest in drawing of all kinds. Art museums are exhibiting drawings both on their own and as part of an exhibition. Drawing is being revived as a major component of fine arts studies in art colleges and universities. In England, the Big Draw, https://thebigdraw.org, has done much to raise the awareness of importance of drawing. In addition to an active website it also has an annual festival. The Big Draw also publishes a series of small information books for primary and secondary teachers.

Loughborough University in England have a dedicated research center for drawing and visualization research called TRACEY; https://www.lboro.ac.uk/research/tracey/. TRACEY's aim is to stimulate, host, and publish diverse perspectives on drawing and visualization to and for a community of researchers, practitioners, educators and students. However, most of its research and its focus is on adult students and professions.

Visual art practices evolve to reflect the social and political landscapes of the times. Today there is a wide range of visual art genres that include environmental, gender, ethnicity, social, and political issues. Art is involved with social justice and activism. It can be participatory and performative. Art has become multidisciplinary and makes use of multimedia. The presentation of art has grown to include things like installation, video, conceptualism, social sculpture, earthworks, or a happening. Contemporary art often holds up a critical reflection of the world from diverse perspectives.

Art in early childhood is out of touch with visual art in the twenty-first century. Being an artist today demands approaches, processes, and presentations that go beyond the aesthetics of paintings hung in a gallery. However, contemporary art practices and presentations are not often reflected in our texts and teachings for art in early childhood. We are either seduced by a plethora of superficial process art activities or crafts that tend to be prescriptive. In our art texts, we are still talking about and using the elements and principles of design like line, shape, and color. We are still using old examples of modernist art genres from previous centuries. Art in early childhood seems to be stuck at the Impressionists era, and books for children and lesson plans about Monet, van Gogh, and Matisse abound.

But our world is awash with art, and knowing how to read and interact with art is critical. Symbolic images are probably more prevalent today than they have been at any time previously. Interfaces with technology tend to be image-based, while media such as film, television, and the internet that carry current ideas and information are also primarily image based. Acknowledging this image-rich, lived experience of children in learning environments is important if children are to see learning environments as relevant to their experiences outside the classroom.

The education department at Tate Modern has recognized that art audiences need a new framework or lens through which they can view and interpret contemporary art (see Charman and Ross 2002). However, at this time, nothing comparable has been developed for early childhood to fill the gap.

This book presents new ways of looking at art that are not only congruent with early childhood philosophy but also more realistically reflect the work of contemporary artists. I believe I can provide a solid socio-cultural theoretical framework that matches early childhood philosophy. As an artist and an educator, I believe I can bring some insights to the processes involved in doing art that are congruent with early childhood practice.

This has been a selective review of the visual arts in early childhood. However, it gives a good foundation for the ideas and theories that will be discussed in the following chapters. It is encouraging to find that interest in the arts for young children is growing and that there is an increasing appreciation for drawing as an essential skill and a valuable component of education.

I host the website for the International Art in Early Childhood Research Journal, which also features other visual arts projects. The website provides information about the journal's Biennial Art in Early Childhood Conference. It is home to a practitioners Zine and has links to interesting blogs and sites. It also offers open access to five beautiful and interactive eBooks about the visual arts. The website is: artinearlychildhood.org

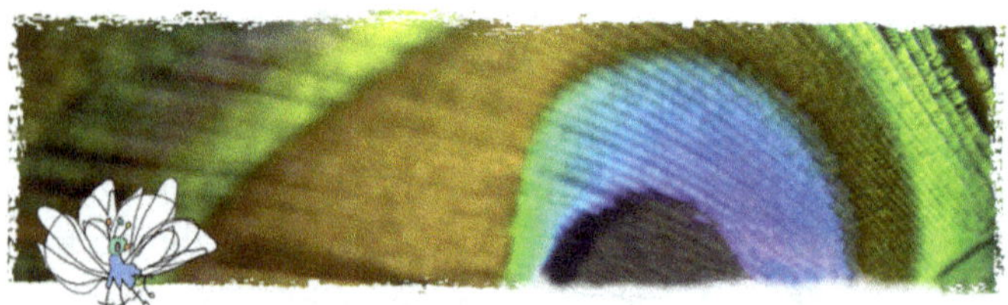

There's an Elephant
in the Room

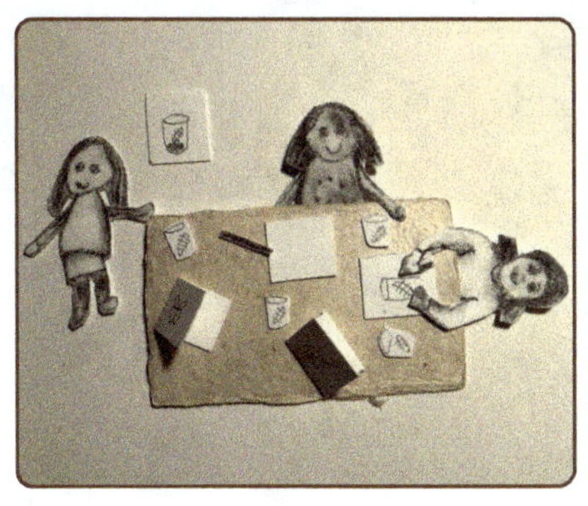

The social construction of knowledge: Watching butterflies

I begin with a narrative to introduce you to a few of Vygotsky's theories in a way that is easily accessible and will hopefully resonate with you. I want to tell you about Jenn, a child in my preschool, and how she taught me so much about socio-cultural theory.

When analyzing children's drawing processes, my focus was not on the level at the which children perform but rather on the methods or the process by which that performance is achieved. I was interested in why they draw and what children bring to the task, their interactions with their environment, and how they work to solve the problems or questions they encounter.

I was particularly interested in the role drawing might play in the children's construction of knowledge. I kept a record of Jenn's participation in these events and examined her drawing from a Vygotskyan socio-cultural perspective (Vygotsky 1962, 1978, 1997). As I observe and reflect on Jen's drawing from a socio-cultural perspective I am looking at more than just the drawing. I am looking at everything that is happening around and with the drawing: who is drawing with her and how they interact, what she is doing and saying, what happens outside of the drawing context, and what are the cultural influences on her drawing. By sharing this record of Jenn's drawing events, I hope to show how drawing can mediate new understanding and become a powerful tool for learning for young children.

Drawing Painted Lady Butterflies

Four-and-a-half-year-old Jenn was one of twenty-four children in my kindergarten class in western Canada (where kindergarten is the year before formal school begins). We were studying the growth and development of Painted Lady butterflies as they progress from tiny caterpillars to larger ones, then pupae, and then finally emerge as butterflies.

On a large tabletop I had placed pencils, crayons, small squares of drawing paper, resource books on caterpillars and butterflies, and small plastic containers that each housed an individual caterpillar and crushed leaves for food. Jenn and several other children decided to adopt a caterpillar and, through observation and drawing, represent its growth and development.

Several children gather around the table to look at the caterpillars. Jenn chooses her caterpillar and, using a graphite pencil, completes her first drawing of it. In her sketch Jenn draws the food at the bottom of the clear plastic container. She shows just how much food is actually in the jar by shading only to a certain level. The marks seem to convey the mashed-up consistency of the crushed leaves. Her line rendering of the container suggests that it is made of clear plastic, while the ellipse of the lid suggests that it is round. I can see that Jenn has begun to adopt some visual conventions to help convey what she is seeing; she knows the lid is circular but adjusts it to her perspective.

Jenn's first drawing

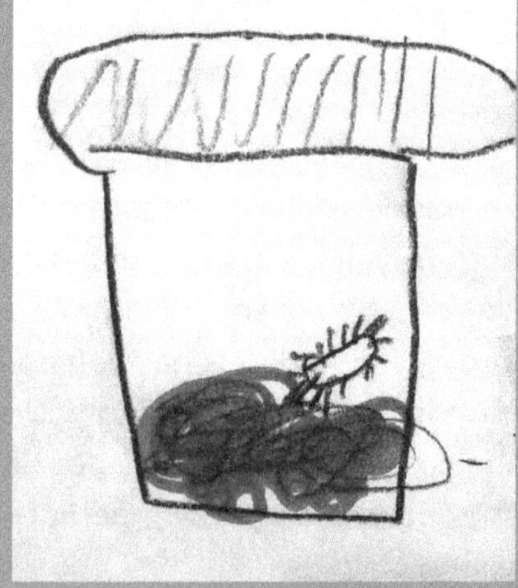

Jenn seems particularly interested in the food the caterpillar eats. Her questions are about how the food was prepared and who put it in the container. She asks how long the food will last and how much caterpillars eat each day. She speculates about a mother caterpillar who might have left food for her baby. Jenn discusses her ideas with other children around the table and hears many different predictions and ideas about the caterpillar's food. She finds no clear-cut answers to her questions in the resource books, but she seems intrigued that each species prefers a different kind of leaf and that the butterfly knows which leaf to lay her eggs on.

I explain to the children that the food was sent in a container with the baby caterpillars and that the person who sent it knew the right kind of crushed leaves and just the right amount to feed the caterpillars. With green marker, Jenn adds color to the food and then draws the caterpillar's head down eating it. She draws the caterpillar larger than it actually is and positions its many legs along the whole length of the body.

I wonder if her questions about how much food the caterpillar needs come from her noticing that there is more food than caterpillar.

Jenn brings her own unique experiences, beliefs, assumptions, and values to the event. She also brings the beliefs, assumptions, and values of those with whom she has had meaningful contact with throughout her life. As Vygotsky suggests, "Thinking, you see, denotes nothing less than the participation of all our previous experience in the resolution of a current problem" (Vygotsky 1997:175). She notices representations by other children and in the resource books, seeing suggestions and ideas that are different than her own and rendered in a different way. During this shared process it seems that Jenn has elaborated and transformed some of her understanding of the caterpillar's eating habits. In this context, she draws on multiple sources of assistance and, with her drawing, in Vygotsky's words, she creates "a temporarily shared social world, a state of intersubjectivity" (Vygotsky 1985:161). This is a transformative process that takes place in a social context. In other words, she adapts and changes some of her original thinking and ideas to accommodate the new ones she learns from other sources. Her drawing is both the mediator and the record of this process.

Three days later, before working on her next drawing of the caterpillar, Jenn re-examines the previous drawing in her portfolio. As she looks at her drawing she reviews aloud for herself her cumulative knowledge about the caterpillar. She uses her first drawing as a point of reference that assists her review; she takes stock of what she has done and learned. This helps her with her comparison of the caterpillar's previous state and what it looks like now.

I hear from her comments that she notices the caterpillar is much bigger now. She also comments on a couple of tiny, black, hairy deposits in the container. The child sitting next to her has the same deposits in her jar. Together they discuss what they might be. They then ask me what I think they are and together we all look at a reference book that tells the progressive story of the caterpillar's growth. Together we read that the caterpillar's skin does not stretch as it grows like our skin does and that caterpillars split and shed the old tight skin for a new one. We deduce that the deposits must be the old skins. Jenn draws a fat caterpillar that she tells me is struggling out of its skin, while her peer draws what looks like the deposits of shed skin in her container.

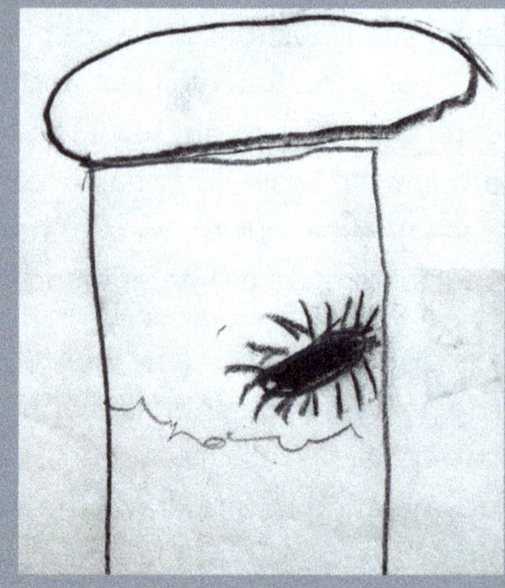

Jenn's second drawing

This time Jenn's caterpillar is drawn with lines that are more random and energetic and give a sense of the caterpillar's struggle. The actual body of the fat caterpillar is dark brown with a faint orange stripe, but Jenn colors it black, perhaps to acknowledge that the skin deposits are black. The food is less prominent than in the last drawing, suggesting to me that perhaps it is not the main focus of her attention this time. Jenn continues to use the same elliptical convention for the lid.

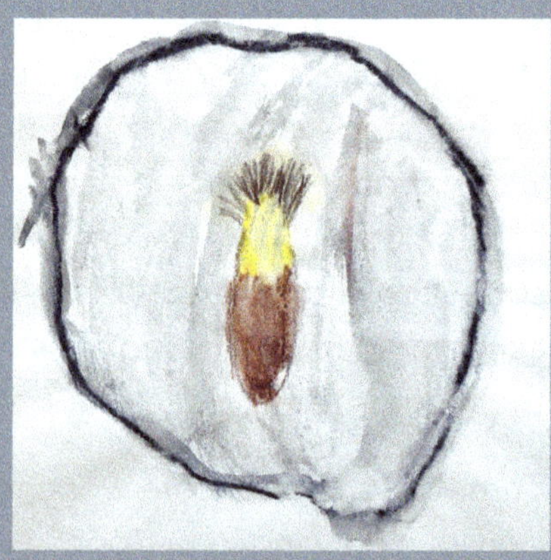

Jenn's third drawing

In contexts like this, I believe, young children are able to set personally significant and meaningful learning goals that acknowledge what each brings to the experience, while they also extend their understanding. Learning becomes not an end in itself but rather a way of participating in a social event to master new knowledge. The knowledge is not simply factual but is also knowledge that grows out of socially and personally meaningful explorations and questions formulated by and among the children. Real questions move the participants to pursue an answer; they encourage their disposition to wonder, hypothesize, and discuss. Some of the best questions seem to arise from activities of current and pertinent interests.

A few days later, Jenn's caterpillar crawled up to the lid of the container and spun a web around itself to stay secure while pupating. It no longer looks like a caterpillar, although what is inside the chrysalis sometimes wriggles and moves. At this stage there is much speculation by the children as to what was happening. Meanwhile, Jenn has been watching and listening as the teacher and some children try out new watercolor pencils. The novelty of the new pencils, along with the colors of the chrysalis, seems to prompt her to try out the new drawing tool. She stands for a while, carefully watching how the other children use the colorful pencils. Some children first wet the page and then draw. Others draw first, then put a wash over the color, or dip the pencil in water, like a brush, before drawing. Jenn asks each child why they did it that way. In her third drawing she incorporates all three approaches.

In this drawing Jenn transfers some of the new information from her observations of others using watercolor pencils into her own repertoire. Through interactions, Jen borrows techniques and ideas from her peers and uses them in her drawing. In the social context of the classroom she constructs new knowledge through and across the visual texts and practices of her peers.

While the chrysalis is transforming, the kindergarten class takes an excursion to a butterfly house to see other species and to talk with an entomologist. The children have a chance to make connections between what is happening in their classroom and what is happening in another context. We see many kinds of caterpillars, chrysalides, and butterflies. There are examples of each stage of development. The children see differences, but perhaps more important, they notice similarities. They learn that while each caterpillar grows and develops in a similar series of stages, the growth cycle differs with the species; each stage has similar features, but each species has its own set of peculiarities. I suspect that this new information will challenge some of Jenn's assumptions about caterpillars and butterflies and cause her to re-evaluate some of her thinking.

The children make many field sketches to take back to the classroom, where we can compare and discuss them. The children's field sketches are similar to the field notes of ethnographers and anthropologists, and we use them in a similar way. As the children review their field sketches they recall more about the visit; the field drawings are prompts for memory, while the discussion around the drawings helps the children retrieve their memories from the drawings. These memories can be shared among children and between the children and adults. This notion of a shared mental process is unique to Vygotsky's theories and is different from a more traditional Western concept of memory as something internal that only matures with age. Sharing stories about our visit to the butterfly house gives us access to more information than we might have individually. My guidance of the discussion aims to elevate and extend the children's thinking. Here I am acting as a mediator between the children, their stories and an expanded understanding.

Jenn's fourth and fifth drawings

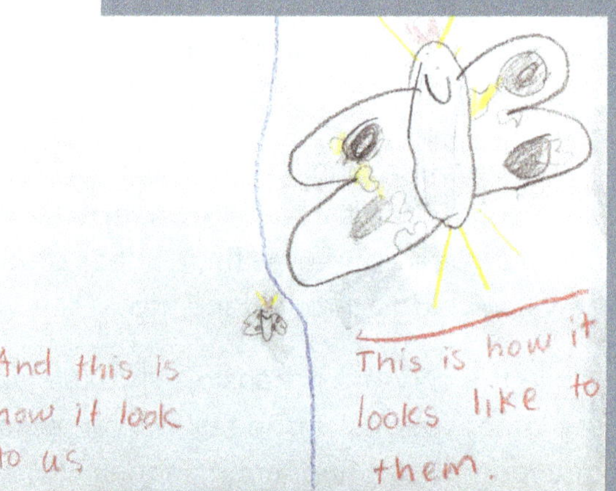

The entomologist who talked with us not only added to the children's knowledge but also helped them understand that some people devote their careers to the study of butterflies. He helped the children understand that care and preservation of nature is something we should all be concerned about and contribute to. Some of the children drew pictures of the entomologist as he talked and would later refer back to these pictures to remind themselves of some of the things he said.

The children got very excited when their butterflies began to emerge. Jenn and the others stood transfixed as they watched the butterflies struggle out of their chrysalides. We put the butterflies in a glass aquarium and kept them for several days so the children could continue to observe them. Jenn did two more drawings.

Apart from the exaggerated size difference, Jenn's drawings are almost identical. I thought that she drew the same butterfly from two different points of view, one close up and one farther away. It was only when she asked me to write the captions for her that I fully understood what she was trying to convey. One drawing is from the point of view of the child looking at the butterfly; the other is from the point of view of the butterfly looking at other butterflies. I learned the value of discussing the concept behind a drawing and was surprised that Jenn would consider points of view both visually and cognitively. I was also surprised that she would use the cultural convention of comparative size to effectively communicate her idea. I was reminded of our tendency to underestimate children's drawing abilities.

After we released the butterflies Jenn seemed to miss watching them. She decided to make a small book out of her portfolio of drawings. She laid out the pictures and sequenced them. Then she made a title page, stapled the pages together, and brought the book to me to read. After reading Jenn looked at me in wide-eyed amazement, as if discovering something for the very first time, and said, "Now I know what happens!" She dashed off to the writing table, where she quickly recreated the elements of her book and again brought it to me. "This happens over and over again, doesn't it?" she said.

Jenn had not only physically ordered and put together the representations of what had occurred but she had also put together all of her prior knowledge and made a huge cognitive leap. She held in her hand a socially, culturally, and historically created artifact that contained tangible evidence of the transformation of her thinking. The physical artefact of a drawing was the mediator and the process of drawing mediated new understanding.

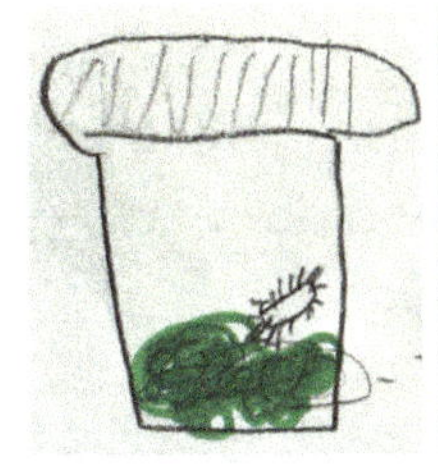
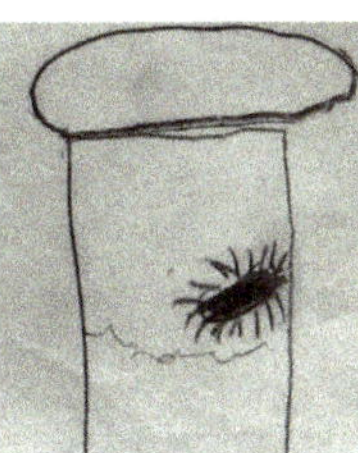
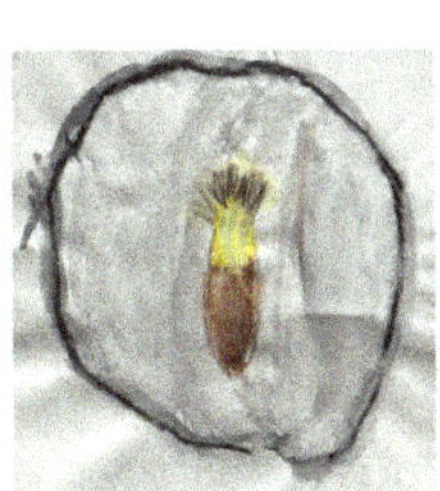
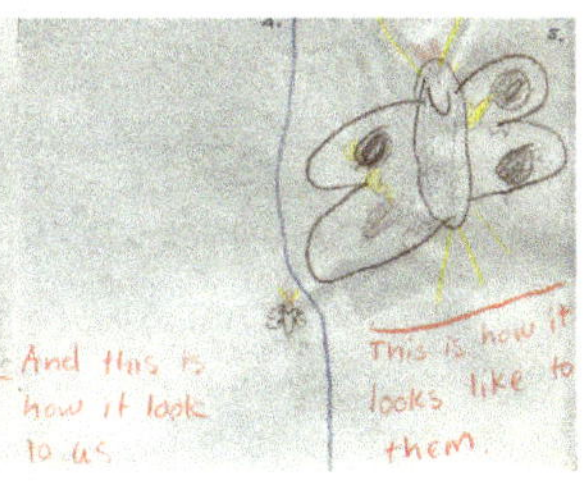

Jenn compiles a sequenced book

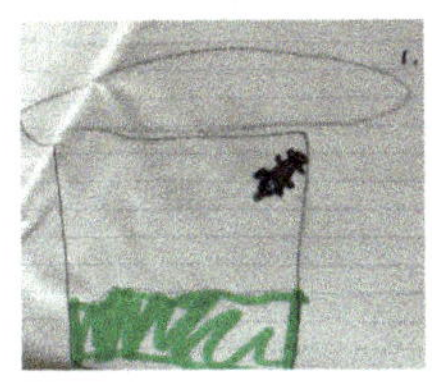
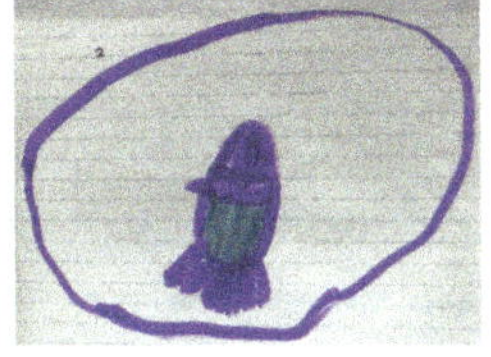
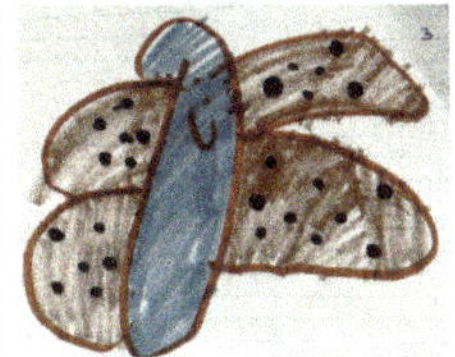
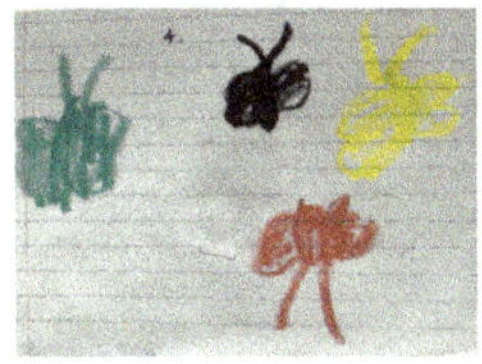

Jenn's reconstruction of her drawings and construction of life cycle

At a Practical Level

I will now unpack the narrative from two perspectives; first from the perspective of what it means for our practice and then from a theoretical perspective.

Drawing helps children make their ideas visible. The children in this story used drawing to better understand the concept of life cycles. Observational drawing was an important component of their work. Most preschool children already have many drawing skills that can be nurtured and extended. However, for those children who find observational drawing difficult or are new to the activity, it is important for the teacher to acknowledge the complexity of the task and support their efforts. Children need many opportunities to draw, reinterpret, and then revise their drawings. The teaching and learning environment must offer support, time, and opportunity for them to pursue complexity in their drawings.

Together, teacher and children can sort through the overload of visual information by talking about what they see, what the important features are, and what a child might want to say with the drawing. Teachers can help identify where the drawing might begin and acknowledge the first tentative marks as good beginnings. Then we can encourage children to look for and continue to add the important elements and details as they are uncovered or they come into focus. The eye has to constantly shift between the drawing and the object to compare the two and choose what to include, what to change, what to remove, and what to ignore. This kind of looking goes beyond striving for realism; instead, the child pays attention to a story or an idea, such as the life cycle of a caterpillar.

For clarity, responsiveness, and simplicity, it's best to begin with plain white paper, graphite pencils, and a good supply of erasers (just as much of a drawing tool as a pencil). I provide these materials in all learning contexts and encourage children to record many of the things we see and do. We talk about drawing as a way of gathering information, remembering, thinking, and planning.

Teachers can model and discuss strategies for learning, thinking, and using drawing as a meaning-making tool. This can be done individually, in small groups, and in large group discussions. This approach to learning recognizes the particular skills and experiences each child brings to the learning situation and works to involve the child in a constructive dialogue with others where the collective understanding and discussions support individual constructions of new knowledge.

Discussions around the drawings should focus on the meaning and information they contain rather than on drawing skill and aesthetic quality. We shift our focus from evaluating a child's drawing skills to considering what a child is trying to learn through his or her drawings. We should not only encourage children to review their drawings over the short and long term as well as in different contexts, but also encourage them to become aware of the many different ways of expressing ideas through drawing. Such an approach opens a dialogue that actively involves children at a cognitive level.

Saving children's drawings in individual portfolios allows both the child and teacher to revisit and review them. Portfolios also serve as an assessment tool and a vehicle of exchange within the wider learning community. Typically, a collection of a child's drawings represents a range of drawing repertoires and ideas that enables us to engage with the drawings at a cognitive level and look beyond drawing as a skill or talent. We are able to see the child's threads of thinking over time, the schemas they are working with, and what is of interest to them through the drawings.

When our focus is primarily on the meanings represented through drawing, we can begin to see drawing as an invaluable teaching and learning tool. Sketches like Jenn's provide deep insights into children's thinking.

At a Theoretical Level

When young children are learning, the relationships between the social, cultural, and historical aspects inherent in forms of communication combine to influence not just what is learned but also how it is learned (Vygotsky 1962). In a social constructionist learning context, learners share expertise in order to negotiate and construct meaning. The learner brings prior knowledge and combines it with new knowledge through their interaction with others. Forms of communication might include symbols, algebraic systems, art, writing, diagrams, and language. When we consider children's drawing to be a form of communication and a meaning-making tool, then the social, cultural, and historical relationship with this meaning-making process demands careful consideration.

Past and present social interactions influence cognitive construction. For example, a child who has been involved in writing the grocery list and selecting the items in the store will have a very different understanding of grocery shopping than will a child who has been sat in the grocery cart and told not to touch while the adult shops. Cultural and social structures also influence the way we think. For example, children who regularly used an abacus had different concepts of number from children who did not. Children acquire the rich body of knowledge accumulated by their culture that, in turn, influences their knowledge and thought processes.

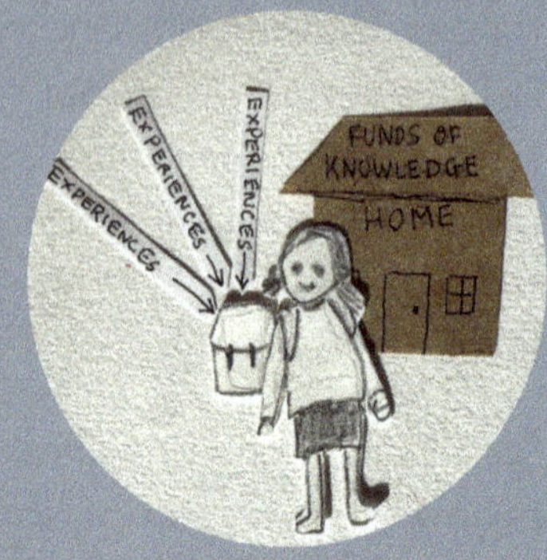

Vygotsky viewed learning and development as a dialogue, with both working together as a dynamic process in a socio cultural/historical context that operates on three levels. While I have separated these levels for the purpose of discussion, they are closely interwoven within the whole context. The learning and development for this group of children while drawing the growth of caterpillars reflects the three levels of social context outlined by Vygotsky:

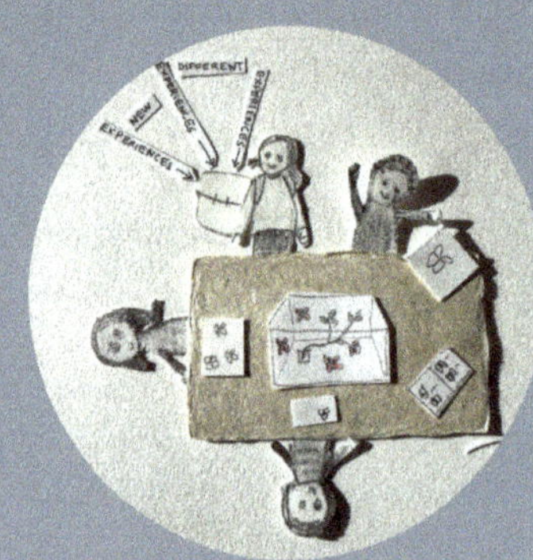

1. *The immediate interactive level:* in this class there is the social context of children grouped around a table in a classroom. They are interacting amongst themselves and with the text, the materials, and the adults in the room in relation to the caterpillars.

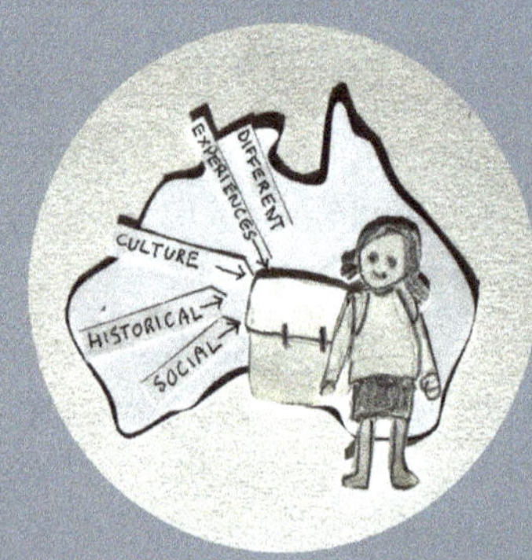

2. *The structural level:* structurally the classroom is within a school, which itself is situated within the wider community surrounding it. Families are an integral part of the functioning of the school, as well as supporting and extending children's growth and development beyond the school.

3. *The general cultural or social level:* the child, the

classroom, and the school exist within a more global context and within a historical timeline of local and wider educational theories and practices.

The immediate interactive level

At an immediate interactive level, there are two meanings for the social context. One is when we construct our understanding through our interactions with others. Less often considered are the other, more solitary, interactions with artefacts and materials in the learning context. Vygotsky proposed that even when we are carrying out a mental action in isolation, we are not really participating in an individual mental process but are rather still operating in a social context. For example, we are using the social and cultural tools of language when we read a book, even when we are doing it alone. Books are themselves social, cultural, and historical artefacts. When reading a book, we are constructing our interpretation of the text from our own experiential base that is itself determined by our cultural, social, and historical context.

I consider drawings to be artefacts that show the child's experiences and thinking in a holistic way. Drawings are grounded in a social, cultural, historical and political context. The process of drawing reflects the social contexts in which the drawing takes place.

Drawing serves a useful function in supporting learning in the social context of the classroom. Drawing and learning dialogues operate on two levels. There is the interpersonal level, where new mental processes first exist in shared contexts before a person internalizes them. Then there is the intrapersonal level, where a person internalizes new knowledge and the dialogue continues at a higher level of thinking. Vygotsky recognized the school as an important site for promoting the shift from personal experiences and interpersonal dialogues to more complex systems and thinking. When children are exposed to other ideas through their interactions with others in their community, they are able to grow into and shape the intellectual life of those around them. While these two levels are distinct, they work together in a continuous spiral of shared intercommunication.

Setting a social context for drawing and for learning ensures opportunities for mutual exchanges and the creation of new knowledge. In kindergartens, social interaction often begins with exploratory behavior accompanied by verbal dialogues that share observations and prior experiences among small groups of children. Physical handling of, and experimentation with, objects seems to be an essential precursor to any in-depth investigation or abstraction. During the initial phase when children share knowledge among themselves, they build an understanding of an object that does not solely depend on sight. The handling of objects brings a spatial and textural awareness. This physical knowledge is an important factor in children's later ability to represent objects.

At an interpersonal level, one of the functions of drawing is to provide a referent to the object, moving the experience into the symbolic realm. A drawing thus provides a point of referral for discussion, reflection, re-evaluation, reconstruction, re-contextualisation, and comparison. While drawing, children talk with their peers about what is being drawn and how. The drawings provide a common point of reference that can be shared among others. When children draw their ideas, others are able to see what they are talking about and enter into a dialogue. As the drawing proceeds, we are able to see new knowledge presented. This knowledge exists at an interpersonal level. Drawing is the mediator for those exchanges, the foci of which are emergent ideas and theories. Ideas often contain physical and spatial information that may well be lost in a primarily verbal transaction. When the teacher engages in a dialogue with the child about their drawing and their ideas, the focus of the conversation should be on what the child is trying to depict and what the emerging ideas might be. A drawing allows new knowledge to exist in a shared state before being assimilated into new perspectives. Drawing is not only a mediator between new and existing ideas but also a social mediator that facilitates a common understanding.

The interpersonal level can be viewed as the foundation from which the intrapersonal level grows. Intrapersonal dialogues are necessarily harder to see and provide examples of, as we cannot see what is happening inside another person's head. Jenn's reconstructed drawing of her book is an example of intrapersonal and metacognitive thinking (that is, awareness of and thinking about thinking) becoming visible through the transformations represented in and through her drawings. The challenge was not for Jenn to produce a more realistic drawing but rather to more clearly represent her ideas about butterflies. As Jay Ruby explains, "The nature of human visual perception is not one of recording the objective reality that exists independently of observation but rather of actively constructing an image of the world that is only partly based on retinal stimulation" (Ruby 2000:216). That is to say, the eye registers only part of the data. The brain forms rapid hypotheses that complement the retinal image and constructs an interpretation of what is seen. Children respond to, and benefit from, discussions and critiques that focus on the message or idea of the representation, concentrating on the construction of the representation rather than on its accurate portrayal of reality. For example, my discussion with Jen about her caterpillar struggling out of its skin focused on the reason for, and process of, shedding the skin and the deposit it left in the container. Discussions and critiques that focus on emerging and key ideas in children's drawing will better foster the use of drawing as a powerful meaning making tool.

Through the process of redrawing, Jenn's thinking about the caterpillar's growth and development changed. Drawing at an intrapersonal level helped Jenn integrate her new knowledge with her previous experiences and ideas. In her reconstructed drawing, we see evidence of both previous and new thinking. The drawing reveals a transformation of thinking that is indicative of an intrapersonal dialogue or internal revisualization.

When we examine Jenn's drawings over time, a historical and developmental progression of information and ideas emerges. Each successive drawing seems to relate to, and build upon, ideas contained in the previous drawings. If we think of drawing as involving many steps and perhaps many drawings in the pursuit of an idea, this opens possibilities for children using drawing over and over in many different ways and contexts. In a similar way, observing these qualitative changes in drawing is important for our ongoing understanding of how children are learning.

The structural level

The structural level includes social structures that influence the child, such as the family and school. Within the structural level, the child encounters new ideas in formal and informal contexts. These ideas reflect the beliefs and values of the family and the wider community.

In the school setting, teachers and children share ideas and ways of processing information. The materials, spaces, time, and social contexts that are offered and constructed in the classroom have direct implications for, and influences on, the learning that occurs. When drawing is supported with interesting and high-quality drawing materials, and the spaces set aside for the materials' use promote drawing in a social context, not only are the children able to exchange ideas about the topic they are studying but they are also able to support each other in the different ways of using the materials. When collaborative work is valued, the classroom is structured in ways that supported this position. When the responsibility for learning is shifted from the teacher and shared among the whole class group, this provides a richer and more dialogic learning environment. When all the decisions about what to learn and how to learn rest with the teacher, this seemed to deter children from becoming co-constructors of their own learning.

The general cultural or social level

Our interactions with social, cultural, and historical artefacts shape the way we learn and develop and in turn shape the way we construct new artefacts. The learner reflects the culture in which he or she is situated. Vygotsky suggests that new mental processes exist in shared contexts before they are internalized, and that the learner is an active and interactive agent in his or her learning. For Vygotsky, the social context is always part of the developmental and learning process. The Vygotsky scholar Vera John-Steiner summarizes Vygotsky's sociocultural/historical ideas well:

> *Central to his approach is a view of the mind which extends beyond the "skull," which does not situate thinking in the confined spaces of the individual brain or mind. Instead, he proposes a sustained dynamic between other humans both present and past, books, the rest of our material and nonmaterial culture, and the individual engaged in symbolic activity. For Vygotsky, interaction with caregivers, peers, teachers and the material world is the basis of intellectual development (John-Steiner 1997:xviii).*

I linked the study of caterpillars to experiences outside of school and the wider cultural community by taking the children to the butterfly house and by having the entomologist share details of his profession with them. Our visit helped children see connections between what they learn in school and what happens outside of school. When children experience these connections they see relevance in their learning.

Visits to locations outside the classroom are valuable if active links between school and community are emphasized. Drawing was the medium of data collection and information transfer. The information collected on these visits can be brought back, revisited, and processed in more depth. Rather than aiming to summarize learning at the culmination of a study, the visits outside the classroom were springboards for further investigation. It was fieldwork in an anthropological sense. Children went equipped with clipboards, cameras, and questions. They gathered information on these visits knowing they would use it in ongoing investigations in the classroom. Fieldwork linked what the children did in school with the community at large, as well as exposing overarching structures in that wider community. Drawing was a critical element in this linkage. While each drawing was individually constructed and contained a personal understanding, collectively the drawings reconciled these more personal meanings and helped to move the children to more generalized understanding of their experiences.

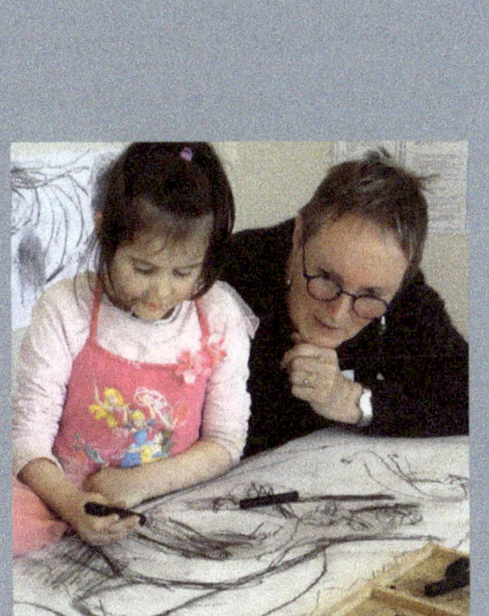

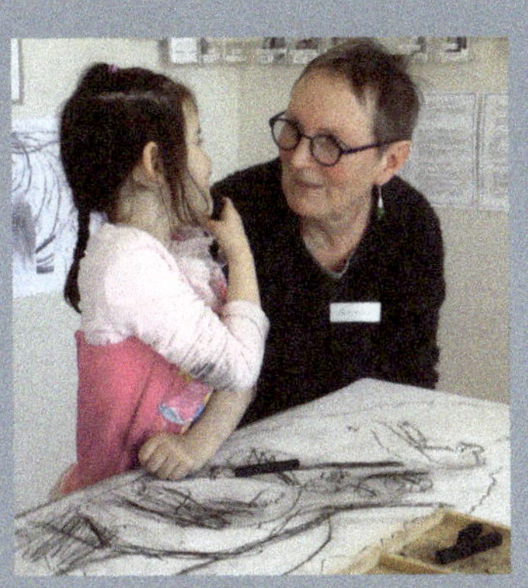

Implications for programming and practice

Educators must pay close attention to the kinds of activities, opportunities, and discussions that accompany children's interactions. It is at this time that children's ideas, questions, and misconceptions are most visible. Drawing help children make their ideas visible. When drawing is one of the modes of exchange, these ideas can be reviewed and revisited by both teacher and child. Drawings may also serve as a vehicle of exchange within the wider learning community.

It is also important that strategies for learning, thinking, and using drawing as a meaning making tool be modeled and talked about individually and in small groups, as well as in large group discussions. This approach to learning recognizes the particular skills and experiences each child brings to the learning situation and works to involve the child in a continuous dialogic spiral where the collective understanding and discussions work to support individual constructions. Drawing functions well as part of this model.

The teaching and learning environment must offer the support, time, and opportunity for children to pursue complexity in their drawing. The focus of the discussion around drawing should be about the meaning and information it contains, rather than on drawing skills and aesthetic qualities. This shifts the focus from performance criteria to a concern with the meaning that the children are trying to make of certain phenomena through their drawing. This approach opens a dialogue that actively involves children in more complex thinking.

While drawing at the interpersonal level helps children learn new ideas from others , it is worthwhile pursuing the cognitive complexity and abstraction that drawing seems to support at an intrapersonal level. This often means asking more from children through drawing, such as asking them to do more than one drawing, keep a portfolio, review their drawings over time and discuss their drawing with the class. Interpersonal and intrapersonal levels may operate in an integrated, recursive, and ongoing cycle, building more complex concepts and representational repertoires. One of the qualities of drawing is its generative and divergent possibilities. One of its great strengths lies in its ability to immediately reflect back to the person drawing the ideas that are revealed. This is perhaps why young children find drawing such a powerful tool. It is immediately holistic and interactive in ways that writing is not.

In order to illustrate further how a Vygotskian theoretical framework might be helpful in providing guidance for the arts in early childhood, in the next few chapters I will describe and unpack the basic principles of a few Vygotskian theories I feel are relevant to art in early childhood. I will often accompany these theories with examples of what they might look like in practice.

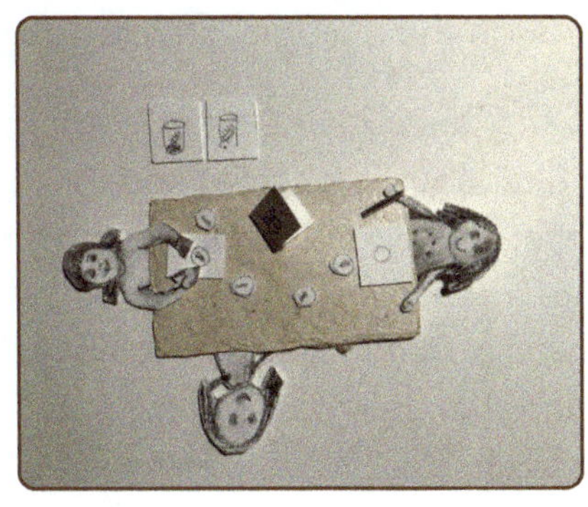

Thought, Drawing, and Meaning

Vygotsky was interested in the relationship between thought, language, and meaning. His most widely read text, Thought and Language, has been analyzed and written about by many scholars and has several translations in English. In this book he suggests that "the rational, intentional conveying of experience and thought to others requires a mediating system, the prototype of which is human speech" (Vygotsky 1962: 6).

When we look at what Vygotsky means by a *mediating system* we find he listed a range of mediation tools such as symbols, algebraic systems, art, writing, and diagrams. However, he was most interested in oral language or speech. For Vygotsky, speech was a meaning making tool that was uniquely human. We need speech in order to think. When speech and thinking come together they can create meaning. Without speech it is difficult to think, create meaning, and communicate that meaning with others. He proposed that it was in "word meaning" that thought and speech join to become verbal thought, and that through the study of meaning making we might find ways to understand children's thinking.

Speech informs thought, and thought is given life through speech. Meaning is created at the intersection of, and through the dynamic relationship between, thought and speech. I have found that drawing can also help children construct meaning. There are parallels between Vygotsky's notion of speech and thought and my notion of drawing and thought. It is through the dialogic interchange between thought and drawing that we get visual thought.

The advantage of drawing is that an image is seen as a whole and simultaneously, whereas speech has a more linear and temporal order as it comes out one word at a time. Drawing is used by young children not only to communicate ideas and thoughts but also to create a sense of meaning for themselves and for others. The power of drawing for children (and adults) is that it closely resembles thought. When a thought or idea is externalized in the form of a drawing then it is possible to interact with it and re-contextualize, revisit, and revise it. Unlike oral speech, drawing leaves a more permanent record that can be shared again as well as revisited. While text might leave a visible trace, it does not have the same simultaneity of access that an image has. Text has to be read in a linear fashion and one has to remember details over time in order to make sense of it. Often with text one has to also translate the text into images to make meaning as one reads.

My work builds on Vygotsky's ideas and my focus is specifically drawing. I chose drawing because it is foundational in the arts. So, while I talk about drawing what I say could be generalized to all forms of artistic representation. If we consider drawing to be a mediation tool, and a language of sorts, then we can start to see how drawing contributes to the formulation of thinking and meaning. When we study the whole—drawing, thinking, and meaning—within the sociocultural and historical contexts of the production of drawing, then we are able to see how children use drawing as a meaning making tool.

True human communication requires ability to generalize, which is an advanced stage in the development of word meanings. At Jenn's initial encounter with the caterpillar she only had that one experience upon which to draw. She did not yet know about other caterpillars. She was therefore not able to generalize or engage in a wider perspective including all caterpillars or look at this caterpillar in relation to other caterpillars. She could label the caterpillar but could not yet make any links to other caterpillars.

For meaning to develop further, the child has to move beyond directly linking to an object to a more generalized abstraction where objects are grouped into categories rather than remaining single objects. Vygotsky states that it is not enough to have labels for objects in order to think and solve problems, but what is also needed is an ability to manipulate these labels across contexts that will allow for connections that promote higher levels of thinking. The ability to manipulate labels across contexts is, however, dependent upon the child's adequate understanding of the concept. The higher forms of human intercourse are possible only when we are thinking at a conceptual level. That is why certain thoughts cannot be communicated to children even if they are familiar with the necessary words—they may be lacking knowledge of a concept that is necessary for full understanding. Vygotsky suggests that a working or experiential understanding is needed, and I propose that drawing serves this purpose well. Drawing helps define words that initially only exist at the level of recitation.

For example, when Jenn made observational drawings of the growth and development of a caterpillar, its chrysalis, and eventually the butterfly, I assumed throughout this process that Jenn knew what life cycle meant. It was a term that was used frequently in class conversation and teaching. Jenn could recite the words *life cycle, caterpillar,* and *butterfly* and could label her drawings easily. However, she did not know that this was a recurring cyclical event common to all butterflies. It was not until Jenn assembled her drawings into a sequence that she was able to fully understand the concept, well enough to be able to transfer the information into a different context and redraw the sequence from memory. She was able to show me how a caterpillar's life cycle was a recurring event. She was also able to understand that this cycle might sometimes be broken. Through her drawing, the concept of life cycle became more complex and more meaningful.

Having a word label for a concept is different from having had the experience of it. It is different to read and talk about the word swim or hatching than it is to do it or be there when it is happening. There is a difference between knowing about something and experiencing something. Some ideas appear to take more processing than others do. The process of drawing can help with the processing of ideas.

The experience of creating a drawing is more complex than hearing, memorizing, or reciting word labels. When children draw they become fully engaged with the subject being drawn. However, when children acquire word labels the acquisition tends to be at a recitation level. Drawing involves all of the child's past and present experiences as well as imagination, memory, observation, and emergent thinking. When children draw they are also engaged multimodally. Drawing is kinesthetic, cognitive, and perceptual. When these three elements are brought together the learning experience is richer, deeper and remembered more easily.

As a teacher I gave Jenn all the labels and words she needed to describe the process of a life cycle. However, her understanding could have remained at the level of recitation without any real understanding. It was through observation, dialogue, drawing, redrawing, and retelling of events that real understanding happened for Jenn.

As a teacher, I therefore need to actively and thoughtfully provide for drawing throughout the program. I need to provide occasions for observing and talking with children about their drawings. It is important that I provide support for drawing by actively responding to their requests for help and that I draw with children and encourage others to draw with children.

Spontaneous Concepts and Scientific Concepts

Vygotsky wrote about two forms of meaning: meaning as reference and abstraction (the spontaneous concept) and meaning as a contextualized personal sense (the scientific concept) (Wertsch 2000). "Meaning as reference" means that the child is able to label a familiar object; she has a name for the object. When an object has a name, she is able to use that name to discuss and think about the object. However, she may not yet know about this object in different contexts. For example, the child might know about the tree in her garden because it is part of her everyday experience. However, her knowledge of tree is likely still at the simple level of naming that tree. She may not yet know what else might be classified as tree

Verbal thought

Thought

Verbal thought

Speech

Meaning

Visual thought

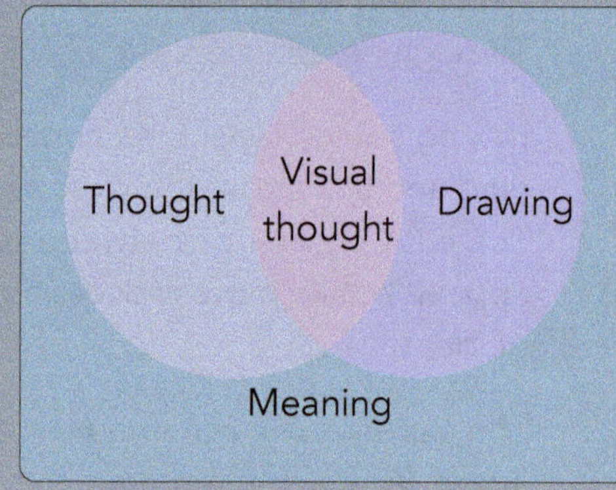

or about the forest, the tree farm, or the arboretum. These trees are not yet part of her experience or context; she does not yet know about these different kinds and categories of trees. When a child has experience of a wide range of different kinds of trees, she is able to think more generally and more abstractly about trees and come to understand that while they are all different, they have some common properties. With a broader knowledge and more experiences she acquires the abstract meaning of trees (the scientific concept). With this concept she is now able to think at a conceptual or scientific level about the properties of all trees. Objects are grouped into categories rather than remaining single objects.

The initial labelling is the first encounter or spontaneous concept. Broader knowledge allows the child to generalize and think at a conceptual or scientific level. We saw this when Jenn could label a caterpillar but not make links to other caterpillars. It is in the spontaneous concept that the referential use of language (i.e. when the child has a label for tree) plays an important role. In contrast, the scientific concept begins not with an immediate encounter with things, but with a mediated relation to the object or thing i.e. when the child understands that the word 'tree' encompasses a huge variety of species that look and behave differently and that there are things like forests, farming and logging. With the spontaneous concept the child moves from the thing to the concept of the thing. With the scientific concept, the child is forced to follow the opposite path—from the concept to the thing itself (Vygotsky 1987: 219).

If you consider drawing to be a communication system that supports meaning and that might operate in similar ways to language, then you can begin to understand how drawing is a mediator between a child's spontaneous concept and a child's scientific concept. You will also be able to see how visualization, as seen in children's drawing, bridges the gap between perception-bound thinking and more abstract, symbolical thinking. When young children are able to create visual representations of their ideas, they are then more able to step back, look at their idea, and work at a metacognitive level, where they have an awareness and understanding of their own thought processes. Drawing therefore supports the metavisual, that is, more highly organized perceptual capabilities, which are critical to things like scientific understanding.14

The key to understanding the difference between the spontaneous and the abstract is in recognising that spontaneous is when the child only has a label for the object and a limited experience of it. While the scientific or abstract is when the child understands there is a system that combines many things or parts into a complex whole. The difference between the spontaneous and the more abstract scientific concept is the relationship between the signs the child made and the object; the scientific concept has a system that combines things or parts into a complex whole, while the spontaneous concepts lacks such a system.

Jenn's initial drawing was a simple observational drawing of her first encounter with a caterpillar. However, by encouraging multiple drawings over time, and reviewing them with her, she was able to use her drawings to extend her understanding of life cycles. Each drawing added another layer of complexity and depth to her understanding of the life cycle of a butterfly. Had I not provided drawing materials, the children would have just observed the caterpillars at a superficial level with little opportunity for comparison or reflection to create meaning. Drawing supported the thinking and meaning-making process.

Concepts stand in a different relationship to the object when they exist outside a system than when they enter one. The relationship of the word flower to the object is completely different for the child who does not yet know the words rose, violet, or lily than it is for the child who does. Outside a system, the only possible connections between concepts are those that exist between the objects themselves, that is, empirical connections (those rooted in observation or experience), like seeing two flowers are the same color. A system mediates the concept's relationship to the object through its relationship to other concepts. A different relationship between the concept and the object develops and connections between concepts beyond the empirical level become possible. Each drawing Jenn did was a visual representation of a concept she was forming. Laying out and reviewing her drawings allowed her to see her different concepts all together. She was then able to make connections between concepts and come to the realisation that a life cycle was a sequential and recurring event.

The following table summarizes the relationship between a spontaneous concept and a scientific concept. It is important to note that, while I separated these two concepts to better understand them, in fact they work in continuous dialogue with each other. Scientific concepts reach down into spontaneous concepts and pull them upward, while spontaneous concepts reach up into scientific concepts and pull themselves up.

Spontaneous Concept	Scientific Concept
• Referential relationship between signs and objects • First or immediate encounter with an experience • Referential use of language • The child moves from the thing to the concept • Absence of a system • Empirical connections between objects	• Increasing generalization and abstraction • Mediated relation to the object • Objects grouped into categories • Child moves from the concept to the thing • ystem in place • More-than-empirical connections between concepts become possible

Drawing plays an important role in focusing children's attention on the spontaneous concept as well as allowing them to make connections between concepts. A drawing will often contain and make visible the essence of an idea or concept. When these exist outside of the child, the child can then work with an idea in relation to other ideas.

When a child makes a drawing I get to see something of the child's thinking or what they are paying attention to. A drawing provides a context for discussing the focus and intent of the child. This drawing-mediated discussion can help the child to think more deeply about the object and make connections not only to their other drawings but also to other children's drawings and ideas. Drawing supports the development of more elaborate ideas. When children are drawing I am present and alert to what it is they are trying to do. It is through discussions with children in a social settings that ideas are formulated and shared.

It is through the formation of ideas, or the expression of those ideas, that we can bring something more clearly into a person's consciousness. Drawing can mediate between a child's spontaneous and scientific concepts and be the leading activity in development. There is a strong role for drawing supporting higher mental functions.

Higher Mental Functions: Collaborating and Communicating

Vygotsky considered the shift from everyday concepts to scientific concepts important in the formation of higher mental functions (Vygotsky 1978). Children acquire cultural tools, which are handed to them by more experienced members of society. As a conscious, symbol-mediated activity, drawing is a cultural tool that can strengthen higher intellectual abilities like focused attention, deliberate memory, and logical thought.

Higher mental functions exist for some time in a distributed or "shared" form before being internalized. When drawing is used in a collaborative and communicative manner it exists at an interpersonal level and can assist this task of distribution or sharing. The distributed, or shared, form requires a concept to exist in an external frame so that learners can access help from more experienced others. When Jenn was drawing the development of her caterpillar she was able to watch what other children were doing and use some of their ideas and methods in her own drawing. She was not limited to what she already knew. She was able to use the collective knowledge and skills of those around her. If I had isolated Jenn at a painting easel or her own desk in a row, she would not easily have been able to take advantage of the collective knowledge and skills of her peers.

When children have acquired a certain competency with a cultural tool, such as drawing, then they are able to use it independently at an intrapersonal level to develop new categories and concepts for themselves. Communication between concepts and ideas then also becomes possible through an intrapersonal dialogue with drawing. Drawing becomes a metacognitive tool. This progression from an interpersonal dialogue to an intrapersonal dialogue with drawing might be considered part of the law of the development of higher mental functions.

If adults consider drawing to be an independent creative activity that they must not interfere with, then they are unwilling to facilitate the collaborative use of drawing. The shift from interpersonal to intrapersonal is compromised. When this happens, children miss out on a path to higher mental functioning and a wonderful learning opportunity. Jenn would not easily have been able to pursue her exploration of life cycles. Rather, children should be assisted in acquiring a certain competency with a cultural tool that is part of the development of higher mental functions and a powerful way of meaning making for them.

Drawing shadows

I want to tell you about a group of children who were drawing shadows. This study of shadows evolved out of a study of torches (flashlights). When the children had worked with the torches, they had noticed not only the different qualities of light created by the torches but also the different shadows that happened when they pointed the light at objects. Armed with clipboards and pencils they began their exploration of shadows by going outside to find, observe, and draw them.

Al's drawing of the bike rack and shadow

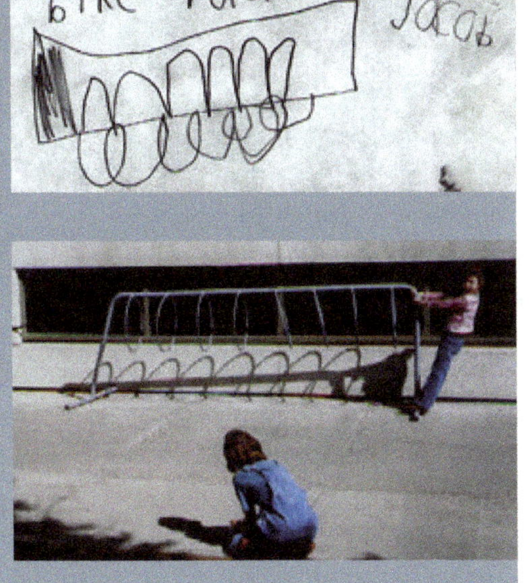

Al's exploration of shadows

Al drew the shadow of the bike rack. He said, "I drew the bike rack because the shadow looked so different from the rack." He wondered why that would happen. He was surprised that shadows were not necessarily replicas of the objects that created them. I noticed in his drawing that he had looped the shadows like a continuous row of 'e's, while his drawing of the rack looked more like a row of 'n's.

Referring to both his drawing and the bike rack, he showed me how the hoops of the bike rack had been separate circles that were attached to the bar at the top while the shadows appeared to be a continuous loop. Had Al not drawn the bike rack I doubt he would have observed this detail.

There was so much to see that it was often difficult to know what to pay attention to. When Al chose something that caught his attention to draw, it helped focus that attention. Drawing the bike rack meant that Al had to spend time looking more closely at it. In the process of making the drawing, he became more aware of what it was that first caught his attention and his drawing provided a means for him to articulate the discovery he made about shadows.

Al's motivation for drawing the bike rack and its shadows was to discover more about the nature of shadows. In this context, drawing was a meaning making tool. Al began with a spontaneous encounter and concept and through his drawing moved to a higher level of thinking. Al discovered that shadows were not necessarily replicas of the objects that created them. Drawing acted as the mediation tool that allowed for this new understanding. When I encountered Al drawing the bike rack, our discussion focused on what he had chosen to draw and why he had chosen to draw it, as well as what he was discovering in the process. Back in the classroom, when sharing his drawing with his peers, he talked about how he had discovered something new about shadows and how this discovery became clear to him while he was drawing.

It would have been more difficult for him to share this information with others without his drawing to refer to. When shared with the class, Al's observation became part of our collective understanding about shadows. Drawing mediated new knowledge for Al as well as for the other children.

Each child produced a drawing they could refer to during group discussions. Drawings provided a common point of reference, framed the point being made, focused all the children's attention, and assisted the children's understanding of the concepts. Sharing the drawings and the information they contained helped extend our collective understanding of the nature of shadows. Each drawing contained an idea that was immediately visible and accessible, and this allowed the children to move between different ideas about shadows and have access to a wider understanding of their nature.

The drawings mediated between spontaneous concepts and allowed the children's thinking to move to more scientific concepts of shadows. The many things that the children noticed, as well as the different perspectives taken while drawing, helped the children see that there were many ways of looking at shadows as well as many ways of recording information and observations.

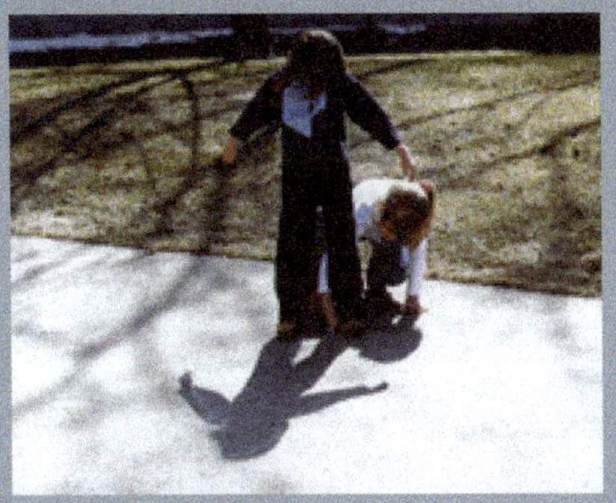

Drawing shadows (a)

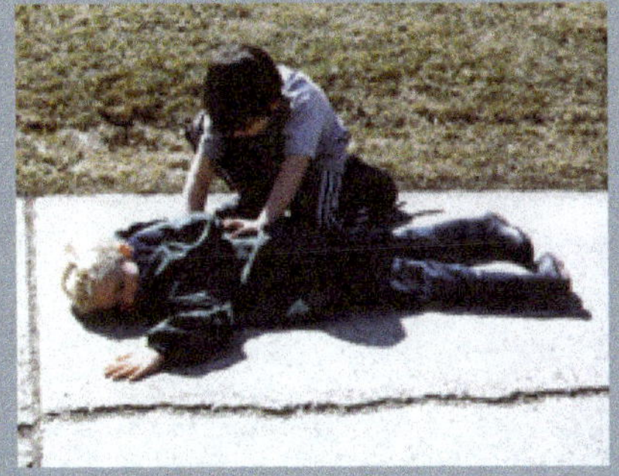

Drawing shadows (b)

Following this activity, children worked with a partner and with chalk to record their own shadows on the ground. Two children noticed that there was a difference between shadows while standing and shadows while sitting. They thought that a standing figure had more shadow than a sitting figure. Another two children discovered that if they lay down then the shadow almost disappeared. There was also a discussion about the quality of the shadow, as some children noticed that the shadow was lighter and darker in places. On subsequent days they discovered that shadows moved and changed size according to the time of day.

Back in the classroom I set up several drawing contexts so the children might pursue these new ideas. One group worked on a table that included several wooden manikins, platforms at different heights, and a lamp. The children moved the manikins around, sat or laid them down, and stood them at various distances from the lamp, providing different variables for creating shadows.

Many of the children's placement decisions seemed to be based on the experiences they had had outside when they chalked around their own shadows. For drawing the figures and shadows, I provided the children with some more responsive drawing materials. Conté crayons come in a range of tones of gray with black and white at the extremes. I also provided erasers and drawing pencils in a hardness range from B to 6B. I reminded the children how to use and care for these materials and I pointed out the tonal features that might help them better describe their shadows.

Al spent time experimenting with a combination of conté and graphite. He then launched into an ambitious drawing of the whole setting. Then he singled out one figure to pay particular attention to and began to draw its shadow. He said, "Look, the head shadow is bigger than the head." He had noticed that there was a difference between the size of the figure's head and the size of the shadow cast by the head. He spent a great deal of time and care to ensure that his rendering of the head and its shadow was somewhat proportionally congruent with what he saw.

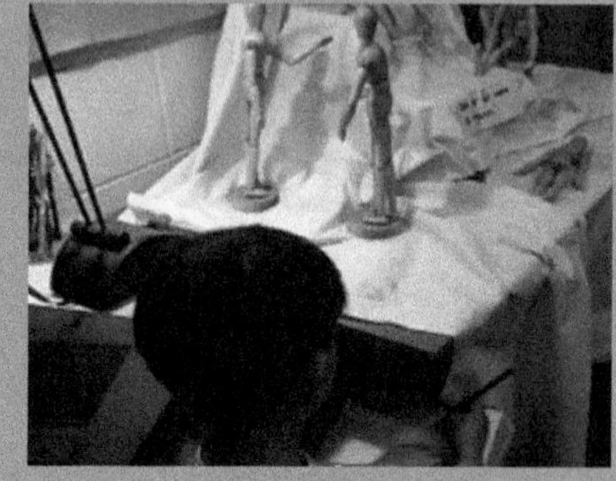

Lamp, manikins and shadows

I could see some conceptual relationships between this drawing and Al's drawing of the bike rack and its shadow. I believe the drawings also helped Al see those connections. Without these drawings, I doubt if these connections would have been as accessible to me or even to him. In both contexts, Al seemed interested in the size and shape of the shadows in relation to the objects that cast them. It seemed to intrigue him that there should be a difference in size and shape between the two. Each drawing revealed Al's train of thought, his connections, and his increasing generalization of the concepts.

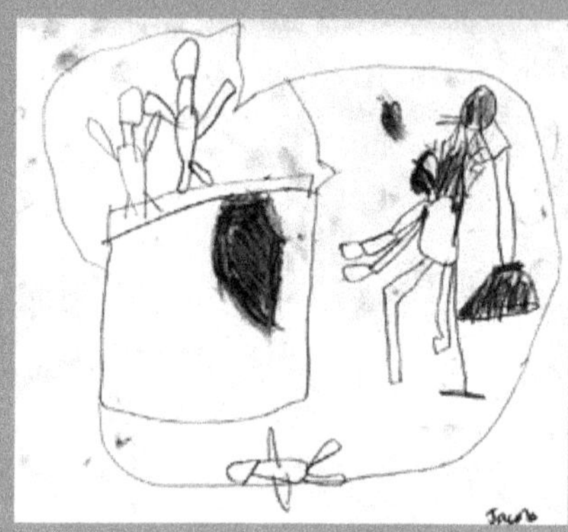

Al's drawing of the head's shadow

Next, Al focused his attention on the different tonal ranges that he observed within the shadow of the head. He was working next to one of his peers who was experimenting with chalks and the tonal ranges she could achieve to replicate what she saw. I could see Al copying many of her actions. There were also several other children drawing the figures, and they were all involved in similar experiments. I saw evidence of co-construction of knowledge in these exchanges of information and the adoption of strategies suggested by others. The children were talking aloud about what they were doing and what they noticed. This is an example of the dialogic nature of learning, where new knowledge is first shared in this interpersonal state before the child gains enough understanding for the knowledge to exist in an intrapersonal or independent state.

I also noticed that Al had moved from describing the shadow with a line to using a more solid tonal approach. As he explored the possibilities of the materials in relation to the effect he had in mind, there was much trial and error. This was the same for all the children in this group. For example, Connie said, "When I put white conté on top of black it makes the shadow lighter at the edges." The experimentation with the drawing materials in this context acted as a catalyst for new techniques and new media that extended the possibilities for representation. The outcomes of the children's experiments led to new growth and development in relation to their understanding of the nature of shadows and their representation. While the drawings were being done individually, the effort was a collective one that built upon itself and initiated new actions and ideas about drawing as well as shadows.

These drawings and the collaborative communication that occurred through and with his own and others' drawing kept Al continually moving on to higher, more complex, and more abstract levels of thinking. He broadened his understanding of shadow so that he was no longer just labeling a shadow but rather exploring the complexity of shadows and realizing his were part of a much larger system of shadows.

When we discuss children's drawings with the class, we are providing a model not just of the language we can use to describe what we see but also what was of interest in the drawing. When our comments focus on the ideas the child was working with, we are promoting the child's thinking and helping them value their drawing efforts as a tool for meaning making. We also honor their intent.

The children's explorations and our class discussions spawned a series of drawings by another child, completed over a week. This set of drawings explores many of the possibilities of the drawing materials and the nature of shadows we discussed during that time.

Rick's Shadows

Rick explained that he had noticed there were shadows on the body of the figure. He tried in this drawing to show the light and dark patches on the wooden body of the manikin as well as some of the shadow shed by the head of the manikin. Rick told me he wanted to show the exact outline and extent of the shadow when the body was lying down. He also wanted to explore how all the manikin's joints worked.

In response to his peers' discussion of the tone of the shadow on the white cloth, Rick tried using a light grey conté crayon to describe the shadow of the prone manikin. He also tried to make the edges of the shadow softer and less dense.

Al's discoveries about the size and shape of shadows inspired Rick's drawing below. Here Rick carefully tries to demonstrate how the shape of the manikin corresponds to the shape of the shadow.

In these four drawings we can see how the engagement over time and the discussions with more competent others supported artistic growth as well as more elaborate concepts. Collectively they represent evidence of the movement between the spontaneous concept and the scientific concept and the development of higher mental functions. The shift to higher mental functions allowed Rick to work at a conceptual level. He worked across concepts through his drawings, instead of being tied to his initial encounter. Through his drawings he explored different aspects of shadows and different ways of representing them.

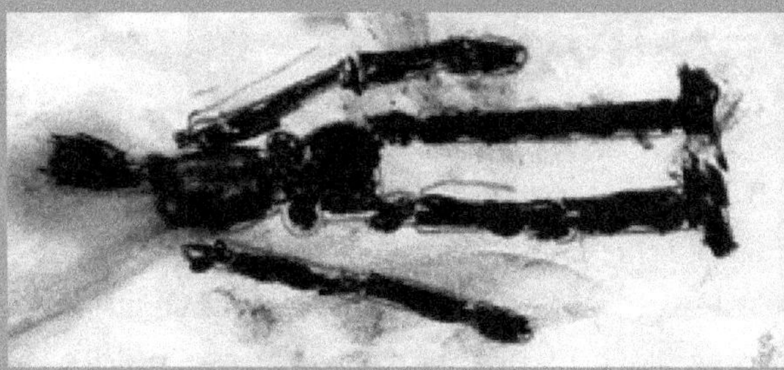

A conté and graphite drawing of a figure lying down

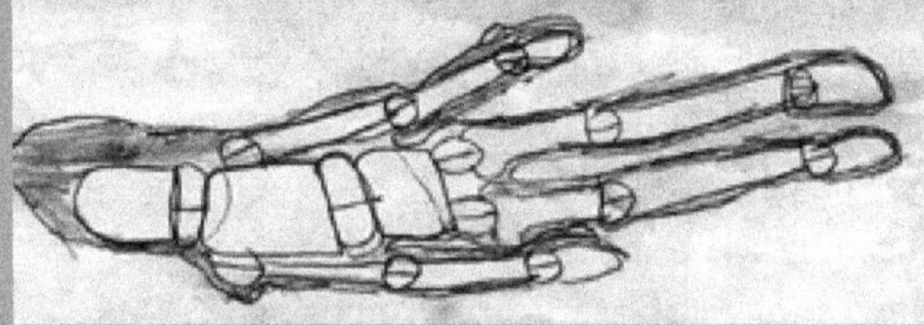

A graphite drawing of a figure lying down

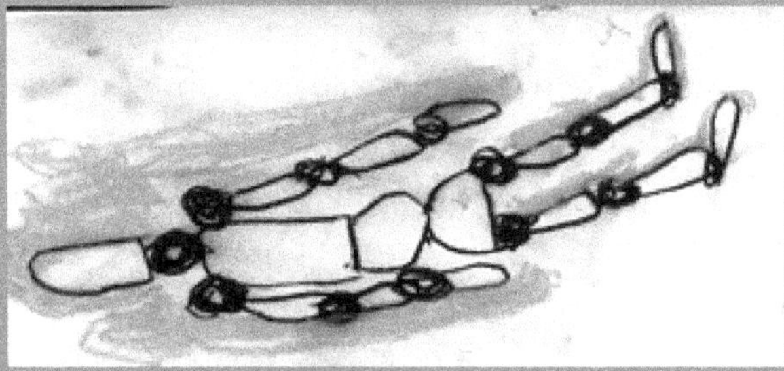

A conté and graphite drawing of a figure lying down

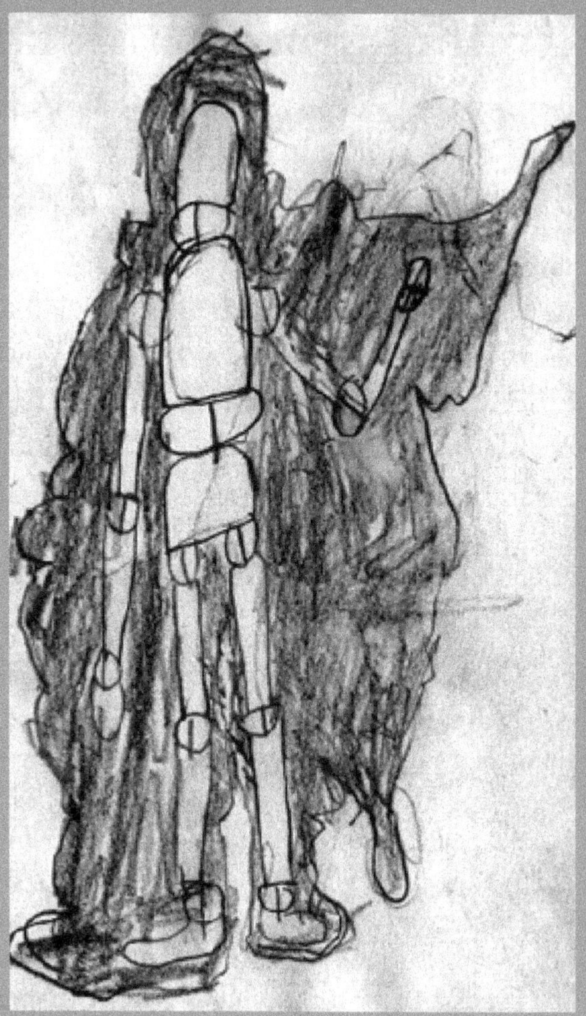

Ricks final drawing of a large shadow

Implications for teaching and learning

If I had just taken the children out to see shadows and we had looked at them and discussed them, I could have assumed that because the children could talk to me about the shadows using the same words as I did that they had the same understanding of shadows that I did. Some children are very good at learning the labels for things, but when asked to explain further we discover that they are only able to label and have no real understanding of the concept. However, these children demonstrated through their drawings that they had a more in-depth understanding of shadows. When I look at the children's drawings of shadows I can see many different interpretations of the concept of shadow as well as different drawing strategies used to develop these concepts.

Drawing involves the constant invention of symbols. Changes in the children's thinking become visible through their drawings. Meaning and understanding are facilitated through discussions about drawing shadows. Drawing played a significant role in the growth and movement between the spontaneous concept and the scientific concept. The collaborative and communicative approach to drawing allowed these children's drawing efforts to develop their higher mental functions.

On a more practical side, as teachers we must consistently provide materials, spaces, and occasions that facilitate drawing and create an invitation to draw. The role of the adult is important during times of intense drawing and learning. Educators in this context are managers and organizers, provocateurs, buddies, and sounding boards. Drawing is a very effective way to slow down, notice more details, and think more carefully about what we are doing. When we draw something we come closer to it and understand at a much deeper level. When we draw something we remember it because we have engaged in a multimodal manner of learning, using our sight, our spatial awareness, and our manipulation of the drawing tool. We have listened to our peers' comments and ideas and tried out different ways of representing the subject. This is a much richer and more effective way to learn than trying to memorize a lesson or filling in a worksheet.

When drawing has become an established mode for learning we find that it also creates a community of learners with a core knowledge base from which big ideas can spring. Drawings from the whole class become a cultural repository of a wide ranging and collective understanding.

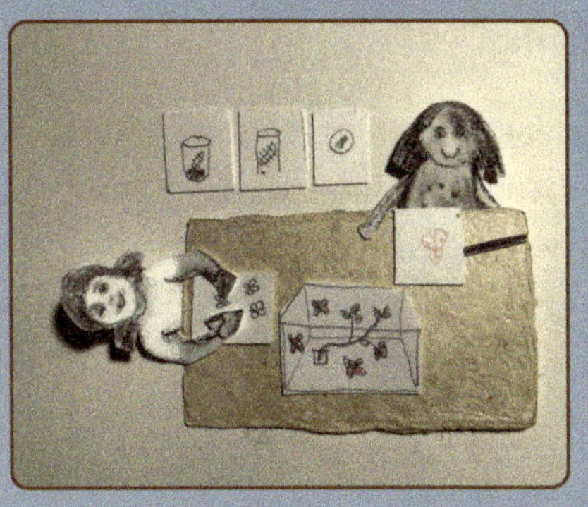

5

The consequential progression of ideas

Consequential progression, in the context of this chapter, is a process whereby the interactions among children and the interactions through and with their drawings build cyclically over extended periods of time so that the understanding of the group becomes increasingly complex. The regular and ongoing sharing of ideas and skills through drawing is an important part of building a community of learners. When children work as a collaborative group, they are able to progress farther and faster than if they worked in isolation. The understanding that builds through this increasingly complex dialogic engagement also becomes a cultural resource that allows the group to progress as a strong learning community. When drawings are shared between and among the children on an ongoing basis, they play a vital and accessible mediating role in consequent knowledge building. Drawing becomes an integral part of the cultural resources of the group. We need to ensure we provide an inclusive context for sharing.

Drawing allows the children to recognize each other's thoughts and ideas, link them to their own thoughts and ideas, and to carry them forward to future projects. At the same time, drawing links cultural practices and concepts with ways of being or actions taken. Drawing allows children to explicitly link previous experience with new learning. It helps children trust their own knowledge and provides a vehicle to work together to jointly construct a mutual understanding. These understandings become increasingly complex as the knowledge base expands.

As young children move into formal schooling there is much pressure for them to represent their ideas in writing, and drawing is often relegated to a position of recreation or decoration. Not only does this devalue and undermine any competencies children have with drawing but it also deprives them of a powerful thinking tool.

I will discuss the documentation of the following project about light traps to better explain consequential progression.

Light Traps

A spin-off from the shadows and torches (flashlights) projects was an exploration of light traps. The idea originated in and grew out of their previous study of torches. Each day, individual children and groups of children arrived at school with new ideas for how to trap light. They often drew plans at home and brought them to school. They made more drawings at school, and these drawings were the medium of exchange for ideas in the context of the classroom. They discussed their ideas over lunch and at recess. They were captivated by the notion of trapping light and the challenge it presented. During class time small groups and individual children worked on the floor with torches and at the light table to enclose light with unit blocks. They had formed a common agreement that all of the traps should be made from unit blocks. Each day before leaving the classroom we gathered as a class and tested the traps by putting out the main lights, plunging the classroom into semi darkness. This way we could better see if light was escaping from any of the traps.

I will focus on just a few children and document how they used drawing to explore ideas in relation to building the light traps. We will look closely at how drawing in a social context mediated new knowledge and understanding for these children. I will show drawing events over time, follow the threads of children's thinking and demonstrate how an awareness of the consequential progression of increasingly complex ideas can be supported by drawing.

Ed's light trap

Ed was one of the first children to build a light trap. While he chose to work by himself on the light table, he was still working within the context of the classroom where there had already been many discussions about, and drawings of, light traps. Ed began by drawing a plan for his trap. His drawing contained elements of ideas from his peers as well as his own emerging ideas. The drawing brought the accumulated knowledge of light traps forward into Ed's particular project.

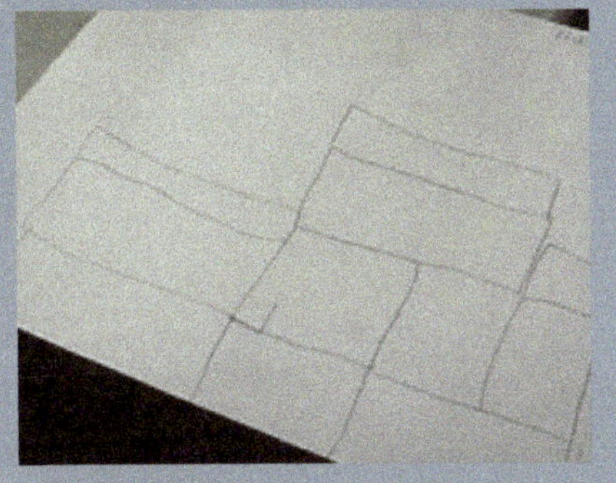

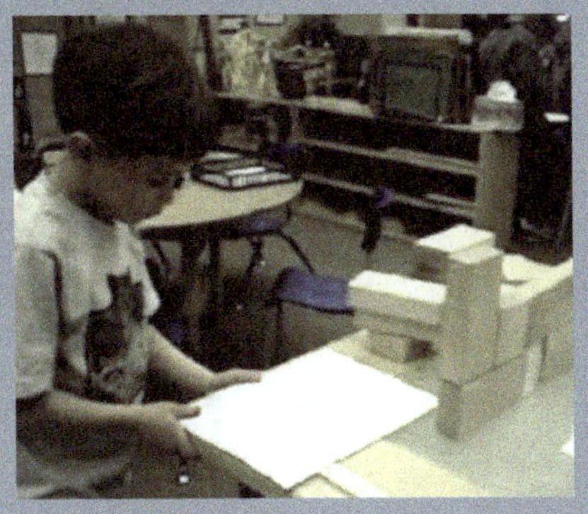

Referring to his drawing plan to guide his building

After drawing his plan, Ed collected the blocks he thought he needed and took them to the light table. Ed's drawing fulfilled a significant role in his knowledge construction and understanding. It helped him make decisions about which blocks to choose and how many he would use. His drawing mediated between thought and action to make his actions more deliberate. Drawing a working plan helped Ed organize his thinking while alerting him to the mathematical properties, shapes, and sizes of the blocks. He also had to aim for some equivalence when working from a drawing.

The fairly accurate proportions of the drawn blocks clearly indicated which blocks he had in mind. He had drawn the blocks touching each other and sometimes had even shared the line between blocks. This indicated to me, and likely to him, just how snugly they must fit together to trap light. Ed's aim seemed to be building a structure that contained the light absolutely without any of it escaping.

Having the drawing to work from seemed to aid his concentration and focus, as the many things happening around him did not easily distract him. I saw Ed using his drawing as a reference point. It reminded him of his original idea. Ed's movement referring between his plan and the building he was constructing displayed an understanding of the function of a plan. It was easy to follow because the idea was immediately available as a whole.

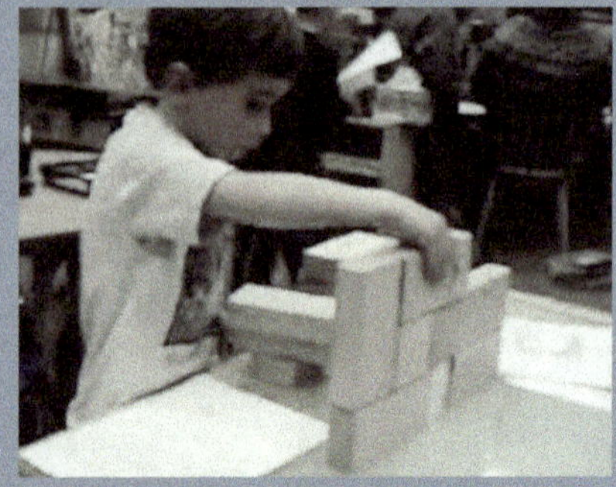

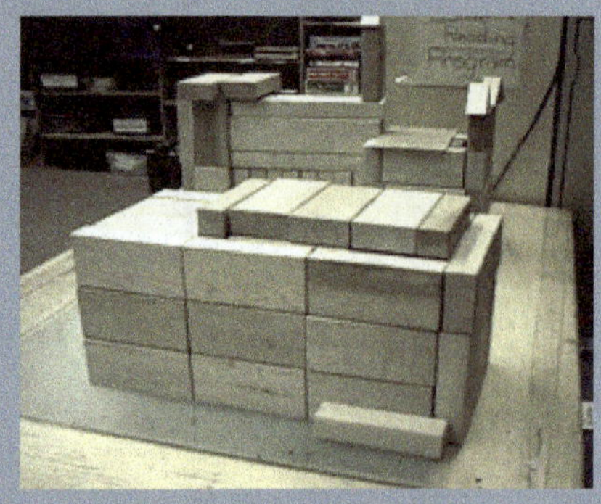

Ed's finished light trap with the drawbridge trap behind it

Ed's drawing was a two-dimensional symbolic representation and functioned as an abstraction of an idea he had about light traps. Within the context of the classroom, the other light traps and drawing plans he had seen had likely influenced Ed's drawing. His drawing also revealed some of the conventions that he had acquired from his viewing of plans and diagrams both in and out of school. In return, his ideas were brought forward and shared with the classroom community through drawing, becoming one of the initial ideas that reoccurred in light traps that were built by other children.

When he finished his building, Ed seemed a little perplexed that the light from the light table was still escaping from around the outside of the base of his building.

Stuart and Anton's light trap

Stuart and Anton decided to build a light trap next to Ed. The two boys sat together to plan their light trap. Each made a drawing of what the light trap would look like. Rather than show the individual blocks as Ed had done, they drew something that looked like a castle with towers on each side and a drawbridge across the middle.

As they drew, they talked with each other about their plans

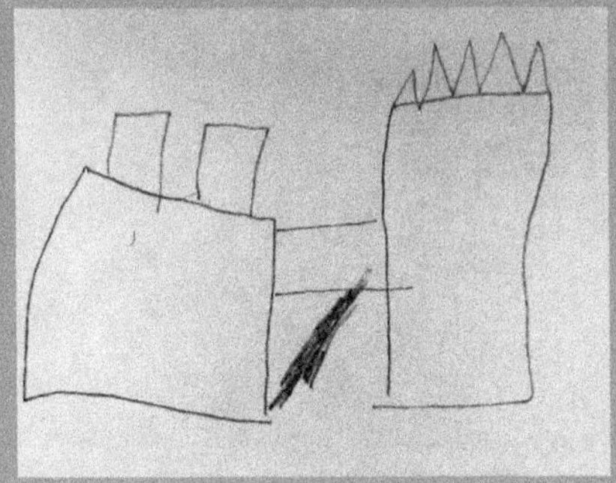

Stuart's first drawing

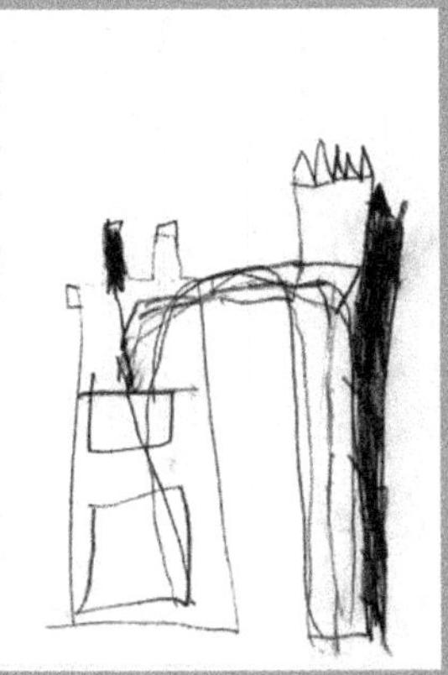

Anton's first drawing

and looked at the other's drawing. The drawings allowed each child to see what the other was thinking. This facilitated a common understanding. This is an example of knowledge existing in an interpersonal form, the medium of exchange being the drawings along with the related conversation. Stuart and Anton were also aware of Ed's drawing and construction and were keen to try to address the problem Ed had with light escaping. This reference to Ed's problem is an example of the consequential progression of an idea. Stuart and Anton gained access to Ed's idea through the sharing of his drawing at a large group meeting.

Stuart and Anton's drawings allowed them to explicitly link previous experiences with new learning. When previously studying torches, the boys had noticed the reflecting mirror around the bulb in the torch and seemed convinced that mirrors and light had to go together. Stuart said the mirror gave the light "more power." Accordingly, in the first drawing, Stuart placed a mirror under the drawbridge. His rationale was that any light that escaped from around the castle walls would be trapped in the mirror and bounced back where it came from. Anton's drawing showed two hollow towers connected by a drawbridge. He wanted to trap the light within the hollow towers.

However, Stuart pointed out that the light could only travel successfully up one tower because the other had windows in it and the light would escape. Stuart suggested a mirror be placed in the tower with the windows. Anton ignored that suggestion and pointed out that the drawbridge was hollow. He reasoned that the light would only be able to go up the tower, through the drawbridge, and down the other tower. There would then only be one path for the light to travel and it would not be able to go anywhere else. This plan seemed to make the mirror redundant. Stuart suggested trying to incorporate the mirror at the end of the drawbridge. The two boys discussed the necessity of the mirror. Stuart insisted that it was the mirror that made the light "bounce off" and "keep moving." When Stuart mentioned "keep moving," Anton paused and suddenly seemed to understand the purpose of the mirror. If they placed the mirror strategically at both ends of the drawbridge, then the light would be forced to travel back and forwards across the drawbridge indefinitely, thus creating the perfect trap. Anton revised his drawing to show how the light would bounce between the mirrors at either end of the drawbridge. Stuart's revised drawing shows the incorporation of Anton's ideas with his own.

Unlike Ed's drawing, these drawings did not clearly show the blocks that would make up the structure. Stuart and Anton seemed much more interested in understanding the path the light might travel and determining where to most effectively place the mirrors. Drawing seemed to help them clarify their thinking about this and move to new levels of understanding.

Stuart and Anton were able to take some initial and tentative ideas about how to trap light and elaborate and extend them through their drawing, talking, and building, managing to build a structure that seemed to them to not only trap the light but also keep the light moving between the mirrors. In this series of drawings we can see the movement between spontaneous concepts and scientific concepts. The two boys worked together to share their existing knowledge, and in the process, they extended both their individual and collective knowledge. The support each gave the other seemed to be well enough matched to allow the transfer of information and

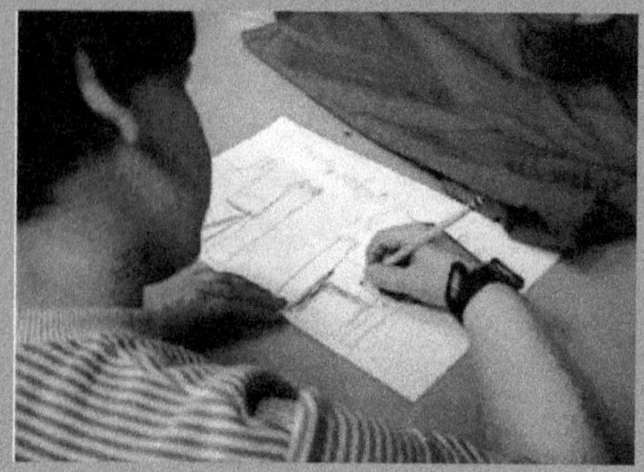

Stuart's revised and elaborated drawing

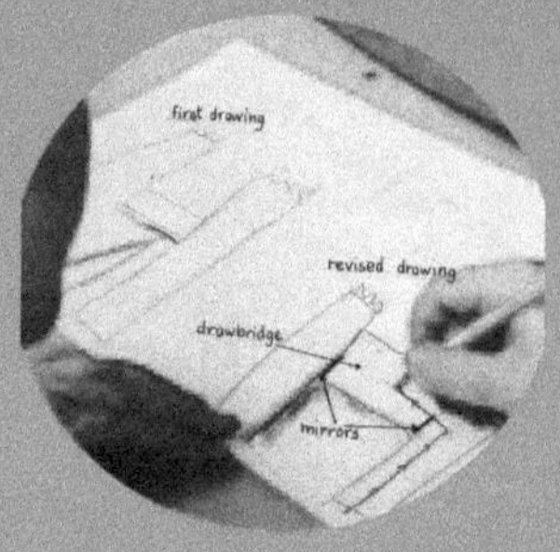

Stuart's revised and elaborated drawing showing the light paths and the mirrors at each end of the drawbridge

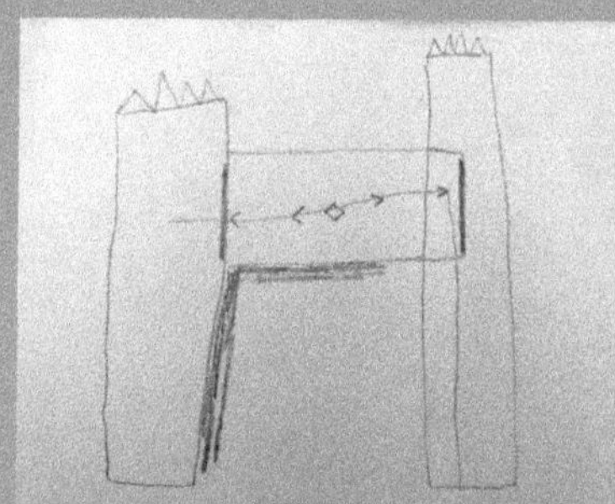

The light is forever trapped between the two mirrors

concepts, so they were able to work as co-constructors of new knowledge and understanding. Revising their drawings after they had built their structure helped transform new knowledge from an interpersonal state to a more intrapersonal state as each was able to recall and retell, through the drawing, the new knowledge they had acquired.

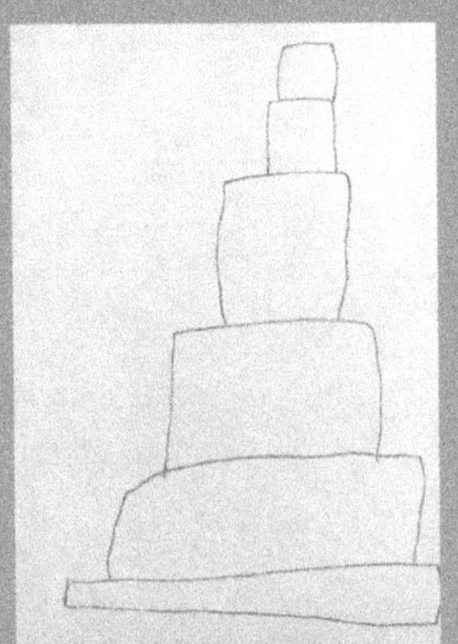

Gordon's plan for a light trap

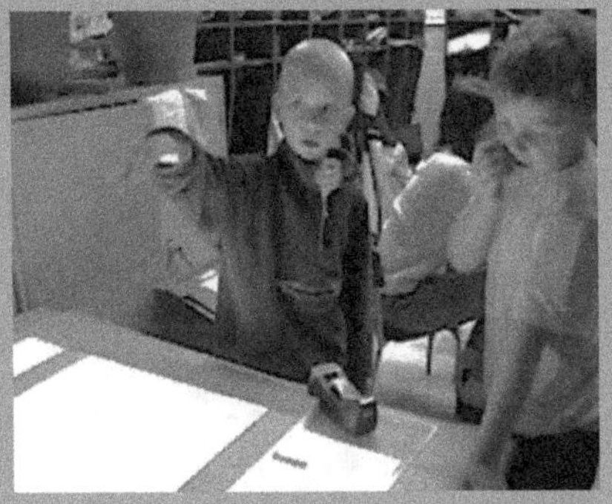

Mark trying to explain to Gordon why his light trap would not work. They use the drawing as a common point of reference.

Gordon and Mark's light trap

Mark and Gordon had been watching Stuart and Anton experimenting with mirrors and now they seemed intent upon putting a mirror in a light trap. Although they were working together, Gordon had already drawn out his plan without negotiating with or involving Mark. He had drawn a solid pile of blocks.

At first Mark seemed willing to use Gordon's plan, but as they began to build Mark became unhappy with Gordon's plan and tried to explain why it would not work. Gordon did not look convinced. Mark persuaded Gordon to sit with him while he drew out his plan. Mark talked as he drew and Gordon watched and listened.

Mark began by drawing the outside of the structure. Beside this he drew the inside of a hollow structure. Then, using lines to show the light traveling back and forth, he tried to help Gordon understand how the structure needed to be hollow to accommodate the mirror inside the top. The mirror was an important feature to get the light bouncing back and forth, an idea obviously borrowed from Stuart and Anton. Mark was able to bring the collective understanding of the community forward into his drawing and negotiate new meaning with Gordon.

Implications for Programming, Planning, and Teaching

The children in this project demonstrated that drawing is a powerful and easily accessible medium for the exchange and discussion of ideas. Providing a social context for drawing, where knowledge can exist first in a shared or interpersonal state before becoming intrapersonal, is an important strategy for teachers. Drawing is a powerful metacognitive tool that mediates between a child's spontaneous and scientific concepts and supports higher mental functions. Teachers need to help children make links across experiences and concepts. Displays of drawings that showcase their ideas and tell the story of their journey provide points where knowledge is accumulated and celebrated.

This exploration of light traps demonstrated that drawing can focus the attention of young children and bring the beginning of an idea more clearly into consciousness. At the immediate and spontaneous level, ideas about light and traps were brought forth and made visible through drawing. At an interpersonal level, drawings allow ideas to be shared. Drawing dialogues among children, often through the joint construction of drawings, can assist them in forming increasingly complex ideas. At an intrapersonal level, drawing can function as a powerful metacognitive tool by presenting an abstraction of an idea, thereby allowing connections between concepts. For example, in this context, the children shared and then internalized the notion that light reflected between mirrors is somehow contained or trapped.

Such linking of concepts supports the development of higher mental functions.

If teachers and adults focus on the ideas and concepts contained in children's drawings, they will clearly see how drawing can support learning. The detail and information contained in a drawing, plus the actual making of the drawing, allowed children to carry ideas across space and time. In these drawing events we can see how drawing brought forward the ideas of the group and the wider community into new combinations and contexts. Drawing became part of the cultural resources of the group, allowing children to explicitly link previous experience with new learning. For example, the children's previous experience with flashlights and the reflective mirror around the bulb was brought to the problem of trapping light.

Tracking the consequential progression of ideas through drawing allowed me to see drawing supporting learning while honoring the intentions of these children. By providing opportunities for children to revisit, recontextualise, and revise their drawings, we can acknowledge and support the consequential progression of ideas within a community of learners.

6

Drawing as a Leading Activity in Development

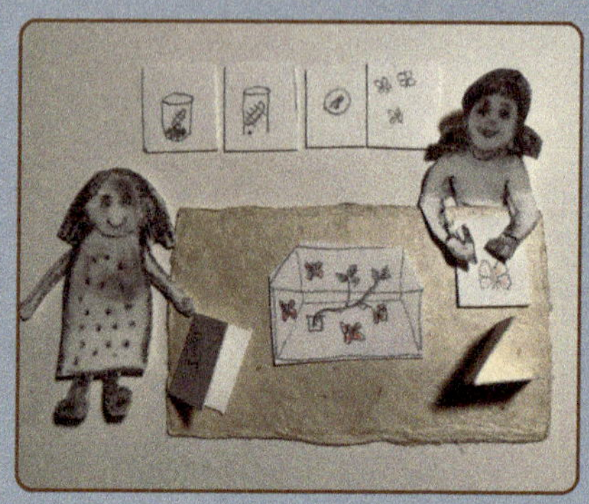

In early childhood education, play is considered the leading activity (that is to say, the most critical activity) in development and is foundational to children's programing and practice. Much of what guides contemporary practice in play has its roots in a seminal piece of writing by Vygotsky, "Play and its Role in the Mental Development of the Child" (Vygotsky 1933).

This short piece of writing, although not fully formulated, is well worth reading. Vygotsky's students and followers expanded on his initial text, and much has been written about play since. In this chapter I will explore how drawing might also lead development and how drawing and play can support each other.

Zone of Proximal Development

Vygotsky has two well-known theories that are integral in defining the role of the adult or more competent other in play and art. One idea we have already discussed is that children construct knowledge. The other is that learning can lead development. These theories become relevant when we take a closer look at Vygotsky's notion of the zone of proximal development. Vygotsky described the zone of proximal development (ZPD) as follows:

> The zone of proximal development is found in the distance between the actual developmental level as determined by independent problem solving and the level of potential development as determined through problem solving under adult guidance or in collaboration with more capable peers. (Vygotsky 1978: 86)

Central to Vygotsky's theory of the ZPD was his understanding of the dynamic relationship between learning and development. He believed that learning and development were a reciprocal and dynamic process in which learning could often lead development. This was a very different position from his peers, like Piaget, who believed that learning and development were two separate processes and that development had to occur before learning could take place.

Vygotsky recognized that children were able to solve problems that were beyond their actual developmental level when a more capable peer or adult guided or assisted them. He also suggested that play creates the zone of proximal development of the child. Play contains all developmental tendencies in a condensed form; in play a child is always above their average age and daily behavior, as though they were a head taller.

This theory greatly changes and broadens the scope of what we have traditionally believed to be within the child's capabilities. It challenges teachers to consider not only the child's current level of development but also their emerging processes and skills and to look toward the child's future development. When teachers work effectively in the ZPD they are able to pull the child's development forward so that, as Vygotsky puts it, "What a child can do in co-operation today he can do alone tomorrow. Therefore, the only good kind of instruction is that which marches ahead of development and leads it" (Vygotsky 1986: 188).

The ZPD is the zone between what a child can do independently and what a child can do with assistance. The whole range of the zone, as well as the difficulty of the task, needs to be taken into consideration when trying to determine the top and bottom levels of the ZPD. That the assisted performance is the maximum that the child can do with help on a given day, and this level has limits. Within each child there will be diverse levels of ZPDs in various developmental areas, meaning that among a group of children the ZPDs will be different.

The ZPD changes how teachers assess what children know and can do. Teachers still consider what children can do independently but also have to take into account what they can do with assistance. The teacher, or more able peer, becomes a co-constructor with the child and works with the child to clarify and extend his or her thinking.

Vygotsky's notion of ZPD is important when examining children's art and drawing processes. It implies that some sort of assistance may be necessary to extend children's art making ideas; a co-construction where the medium for dialogue is visual rather than verbal. The ZPD suggests possibilities that move beyond the more traditional developmental theories from either early childhood or art education that tend to codify what children can do and when. We are more likely to see the potential a child has if we concentrate on the upper end of the ZPD rather than only on what he or she can now do independently.

Peer Assistance within the ZPD

Peers often provide the best examples of working in the ZPD. Here is an example of a more capable peer assisting her friend in solving a visual problem.

Amy is very self-assured and capable, having just turned four years old. Alice is a mature almost six year old. They were working next to each other but not together when Alice noticed Amy was getting frustrated and offered to help her.

Amy was drawing the dolls she was playing with. Alice offered to show her how to draw what happens when one thing is in front of another. "But I can draw dogs better than horses," she said. She proceeded to explain what she did to Amy as she drew.

"First I draw the one in front. Then I have to put the other behind. I can't show all of it because some is hidden by the dog." Amy watched in great concentration. She followed every move Alice made.

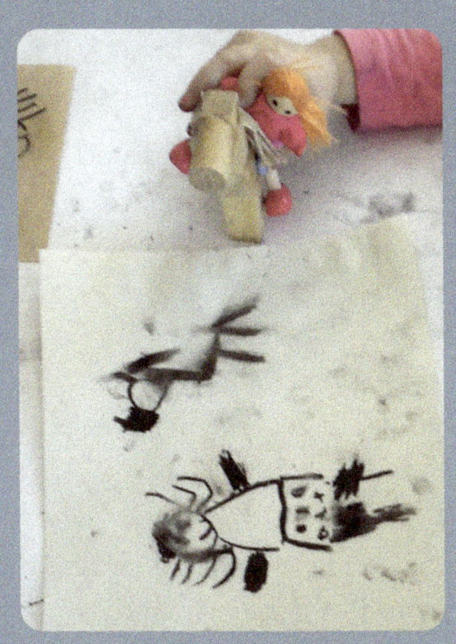

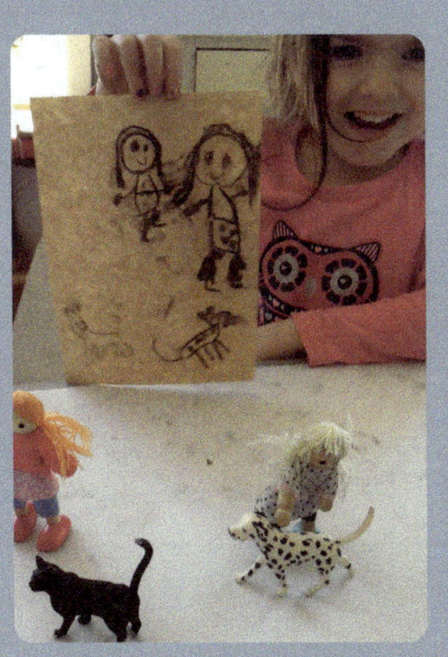

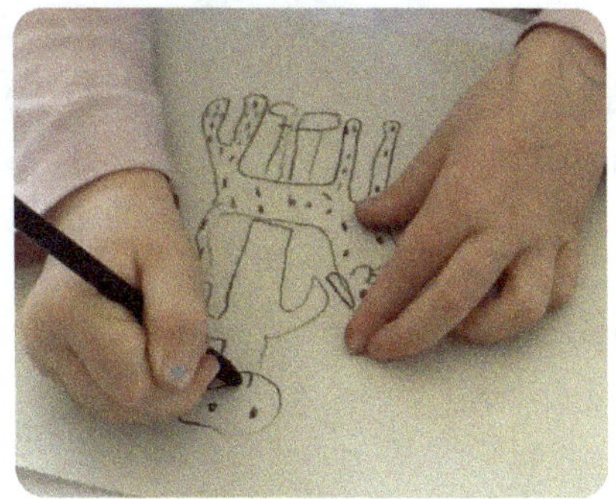

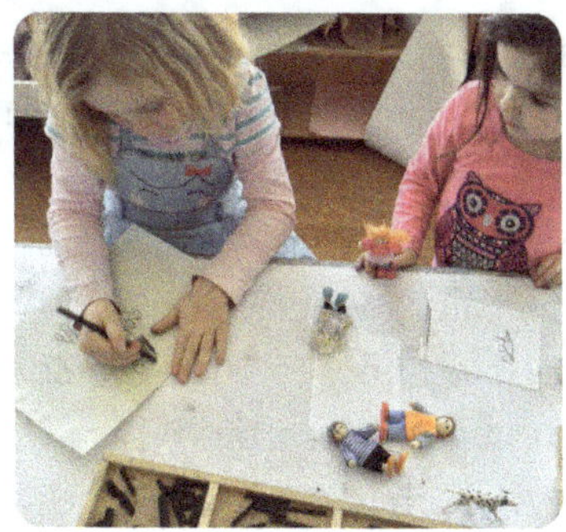

She had drawn the girl and the horse and had tried unsuccessfully to draw the girl riding on the horse. She said that the girl and horse kept getting tangled up when she tried to draw them. She was struggling with occlusion.

Just to make sure Amy had understood, Alice stood the dog and the doll up in front of her drawing and said, "Look, can you see how they are. You can't see all of the person behind the dog."

Amy took the two dolls she had been drawing and held them in front of Alice's drawing. She said, "You know, I found another way to draw one in front and one behind. You just make one doll smaller than the other and it is the one behind." She continued, "if you make one smaller it looks further away. But they are really the same size." She held up a drawing she had done to show Alice.

In this scenario, we can see that defining the more capable peer is not so easy or clear cut. However, we can see that they found each other's upper level of the ZPD. Together they moved forward and engaged in higher order thinking through the drawings. They began by working in the interpersonal zone and then moved into the intrapersonal zone of thinking creatively and providing different solutions for a similar problem. Alice demonstrated how to draw occlusion and Amy modeled how to show perspective. Both techniques are typically considered beyond children of this age.

This event demonstrates that development begins as an interpersonal process of making meaning before it becomes an individualized process of making sense. When a more competent one assists the novice within their ZPD, the dialogue and the learning exist in an interpersonal state. New knowledge exists first in a shared state, between the novice and the more competent one. Internalization only occurs when the novice is able to operate at an independent level or intrapersonal state. When operating at an intrapersonal level, the child can converse with themself about what they know, just as Alice and Amy did. At this point in time the support of the expert in the ZPD was no longer needed. While Amy was not yet able to draw the girl on the horse without help, she was able to draw things at a distance; a technique that Alice was not familiar with. Each child was working both at an interpersonal

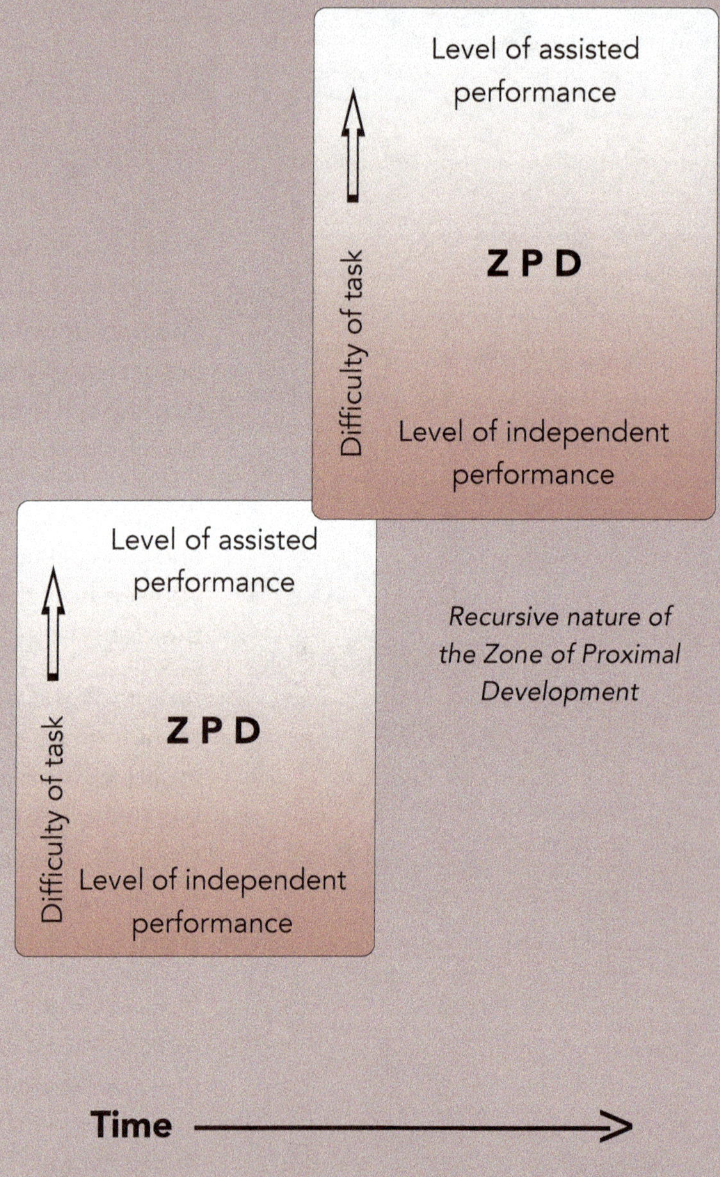

Recursive nature of the Zone of Proximal Development

and intrapersonal level. Here we can see the complexity of working in the ZPD. Each child has different levels of competency in different aspects of drawing.

The nature of the interactions the teacher has with a child around an art making event sets up explicit and implicit messages that influence the way the child perceives the task and outcome as well as its relationship to his or her learning and communication. Vygotsky suggests that ideally the teacher should offer assistance at the top end of a child's ZPD to advance the child's development. Learning leads development and assists its progress. He views the process as one that continually moves the ZPD forward. Vygotsky saw that when a child reached the top level of the ZPD, that former ceiling then formed the foundation for the next level and the next problem to be solved. It was a continuous, recursive process as the diagram suggests.

As Alice and Amy demonstrate, children's artistic development does not fall into neat Piagetian stages. It is difficult to know what kind of support at the top end of the ZPD might look like for individual children. In drawing, when one concentrates on just one element, for example the product or the drawing, it is tempting to analyze it in isolation from the process and the context in which it was produced. Vygotsky's method suggests that the focus should be on the whole and the relationship among the elements, specifically meaning making. If our support during drawing concentrates on making meaning within the context of a particular drawing, as opposed to the more traditional skill acquisition and production aspects, this might open up productive ways of examining the role of the adult or more capable peer. In this event, Amy and Alice were encouraged to share their findings with all their peers at large group time. This prompted interesting discussions about solutions to optical problems in drawing.

Theoretical Responses to ZPD

The concept of ZPD has been of great interest to many researchers, in particular the nature of assistance within the ZPD. Many models have been suggested that offer possible ways of supporting drawing for young children. I will discuss a few in relation to Vygotsky's theories and how they might or might not support drawing.

Performance and Fossilization in the ZPD

Vygotsky scholars Roland Tharp and Ronald Gallimore (Tharp and Gallimore 1988) proposed a model that extended the original definition of the ZPD to include a four-stage recursive cycle:

Stage 1. Performance is assisted by more capable others. This is where new knowledge is shared. For example; when Amy and Alice shared their different drawings that featured occlusion, Alice demonstrated how to draw a dog in front of a person.

Stage 2. Performance is assisted by self. Here Amy set herself the task of drawing figures at a distance, placing one doll in front of the other.

Stage 3. Performance is developed, automatized, and fossilized. Amy's solution to occlusion has become well embedded, or fossilized. However, she persists in her quest to represent the concept. She goes through a process of more closely examining the actions of her peers.

Stage 4. De-automatization of performance leads to recursion back through the ZPD. De-automatization is an important concept for the sake of meaning making.

The notion of fossilization or automation of performance resonates with me. In my many observations of children drawing, I have noticed that children will appropriate certain drawing conventions or solutions that work well in particular contexts. However, some of these solutions become automatised, or fossilized, and are then sometimes used thoughtlessly in situations where perhaps other solutions might be of more value to the meaning making and communication process. One example of fossilization is when a child learns to put a sun in their drawing to indicate the weather. However, the sun is soon used in a stamp like manner with less thought to the meaning it conveys and without efforts to find other ways to indicate time and weather. The child does not think about the position of the sun in the sky or that clouds might cover it or the many ways the sun looks from sunrise to sunset. De-automatization and recursion back through the stages, or a re-examination of the process, could be helpful in moving children's drawing toward new ideas and solutions.

While this model supports and expands Vygotsky's notion of the recursive cycle of the ZPD, the emphasis on performance implies a goal of mastering a specific skill or concept. While performance can certainly be part of the drawing process, this emphasis on performance might detract from the meaning making that can occur through drawing, and it may contribute to a more elemental

Children often spend time watching before participating. I scaffolded his involvement by wondering and talking about what the other child was doing. I invited the child drawing to talk about his drawing. He invited his friend to draw the stars his rocket ship was going to. This was the beginning of a long collaborative drawing.

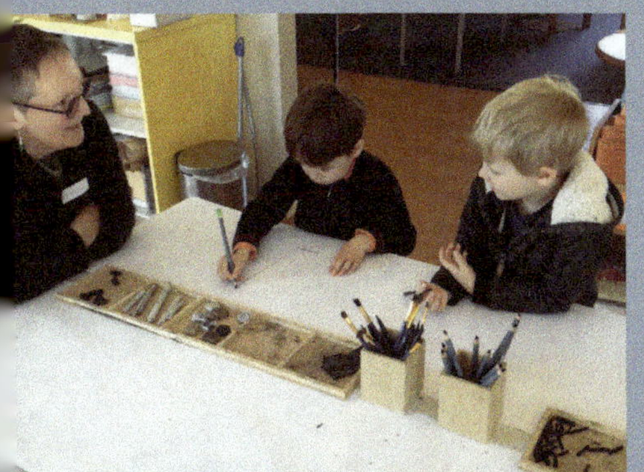

approach to drawing (where the focus is on traditional elements like shape, line, and form). However, if I consider performance to be more open-ended and to involve such things as the ability to raise good questions and solve problems, then some of these stages are more helpful.

The recursive movement of the ZPD has been illustrated by a metaphor of a tidal wave (Zebroski 1994), which includes forward motion but also regressive movement. The metaphor allows for a continuous building on past experiences and continuity. Vygotsky saw this backward movement, or seeming regression, as the time that foreshadowed the reorganization and restructuring of experience that prepares for the next developmental or conceptual leap forward.

It is challenging to recognize this back-and-forth motion while observing children's drawing processes because much of this restructuring is all but invisible. However, this happens in drawing, including my own. Often when I am stuck and can only repeat old ideas, I recognize this as a form of regression and I am forced to reflect on the problem more deeply. It is then I am driven to pull in new and different solutions that move me to the next level in both my understanding of the problem and my appreciation of the solutions possible to me. Integral to this process is a dialogue I have with others about my drawing and my relationship with the drawing.

Response and Repetition within the ZPD

Barbara Rogoff (Rogoff 1990), known for her work on "guided participation," extended the nature of some of Vygotsky's theories. For this she studied the nature of the interactions between mothers and toddlers as well as between weaving teachers and their apprentices in Mexico. She noted a responsive interaction between the more capable peer and the novice. The expert would break a task down to match the novice's ZPD, then constantly adjust and renegotiate both the dialogue and the level of support within the ZPD.

Negotiating both the level and the nature of assistance with the novice using Rogoff's notion of responsiveness is an excellent strategy for facilitating a child's ability to express meaning through drawing. For example, when drawing we are often faced with visual overload, and it helps to break the task down into simpler bits and talk the child through each piece. Accordingly, when Amy asked me for help in determining where to begin her drawing of a horse, I suggested first she draw the legs. When they were drawn, we built upward to complete the drawing.

Courtney Cazden (Cazden 2017) known for her studies of classroom dialogues, also considered performance as coming before competence. She suggests that understanding will occur through doing the task. So long as the task is within the child's ZPD, with repetition the child will eventually understand. It is in the redoing and rethinking that progressive understanding occurs. It is almost like saying that sometimes we need more time to process things. It reminds me a little of Jenn when she was drawing her caterpillars almost every day. At the end of a series of drawings of her specific caterpillar, her understanding of the caterpillar was far greater than at the beginning, as the repetition of drawing the same caterpillar over again allowed Jenn to notice more things than by doing only one drawing. Redrawing the same

Scaffolding

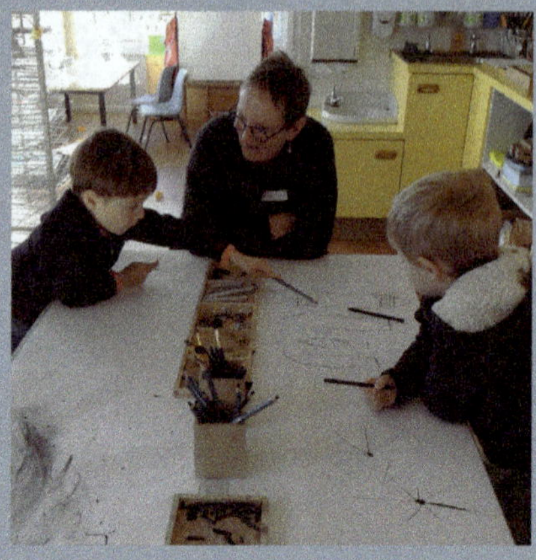

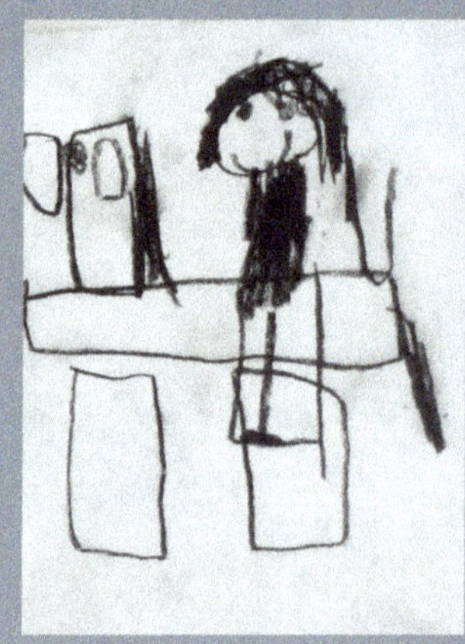

thing also brought fluency to the drawing task that allowed her to look beyond the task of drawing and to use the drawing as a tool for understanding life cycles.

The ZPD has been described as the construction zone (Pollard 2015). It is where the dialogue between the teacher and child co-constructs a path to a deeper understanding. Loris Malaguzzi, the founder of the Reggio Emilia schools in northern Italy, described it as like throwing a ball to a child in such a way as that they will want to return it to you and want to continue to play (Malaguzzi 1993). The teacher and child work together to try to understand each other's thinking through a shared dialogue. They work towards some action on the part of both the child and the teacher. If I view the child as rich in potential, competent, strong, powerful, and capable, this is a different perspective of the child from one that is driven by developmental stages and convergent curriculum goals.

Scaffolding

The term scaffolding originates from the work of David Wood, Jerome Bruner, and Gail Ross (Wood, Bruner, and Ross 1976). Scaffolding is a metaphor for the kind of support that is given within the ZPD. In this context, the task is not altered or made easier but rather the level of support changes. The less capable the child, the more support he or she is given. I have observed adults place a tool in a child's hand and with their hand covering the child's they will guide the tool in the way it is typically used. This is accompanied by a verbal description of the action. As the child becomes more confident with the tool the adult will remove the hand but continue to give verbal guidance until the child no longer needs even that. The adult begins with maximum support for the learning and gradually removes the support as it is no longer required.

The word scaffolding might seem to suggest that the support is of a physical nature. However, if I return to the example of Jenn and her caterpillar drawings, I can see evidence of other characteristics of scaffolding. In Jenn's case, the primary scaffolding took the form of supporting Jenn to persevere in her goal. That is, Jenn's ownership of her caterpillar, and the responsibility she negotiated with me for its care, seemed to be a scaffold in maintaining her interest in her goal of recording the growth and development of her caterpillar. When the adults or more capable peers focus on the meaning or the concept the child is trying to achieve, rather than the technique, it is another form of scaffolding.

Another characteristic of scaffolding is that as the child becomes more capable, more responsibility for the performance is handed over to the child. In the beginning I supported Jenn by giving her access to paper and pencil, encouraging her to use them, involving myself in the activity, and talking her through the process. As she did her first drawing I sat beside her, mirroring the process and talking to her about what I was doing. When she did the later drawings I no longer needed to give her that support. These strategies allowed for a more open-ended interpretation than if I had instructed her through a series of prescribed steps.

One of the implications I might be tempted to draw from working with the ZPD is that all assisted learning is good. However, Louis Moll warns us that this is not the case (Moll 1990). Moll examined the nature of children's funds of knowledge they bring from home to school. He is clear that things like work sheets and rote drill-like practices not only do not fit under Vygotsky's notion of ZPD but may also be counterproductive to learning and development. The drawing equivalents to work sheets are coloring sheets, coloring books, adult drawn templates, connect the dots, and recipe-like instructions. They all come with the same warnings.

More capable peer

Another consideration in our understanding of the ZPD is the notion of the more capable peer. Gordon Wheeler, a cognitive psychologist, looked at paired peers in relation to expert and novice relationships (Wheeler 2000). He discovered that there is an optimum differential between peers' developmental levels that will enable the growth and development of the

What is a more capable peer?

Drawing dialogues scaffold learning. Two children the same age draw together. The girl at the top of the picture has more drawing skills. But her friend generates more ideas that come from her play with the small dolls there. Together they make a good team. They bounce ideas off each other and share drawing techniques. They scaffold each other's learning and for both drawing is leading development.

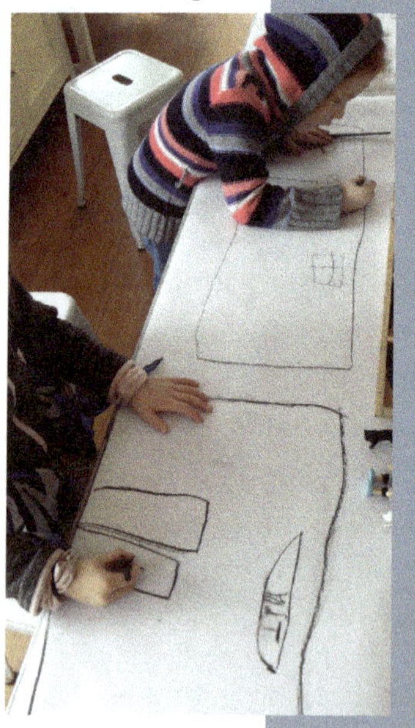

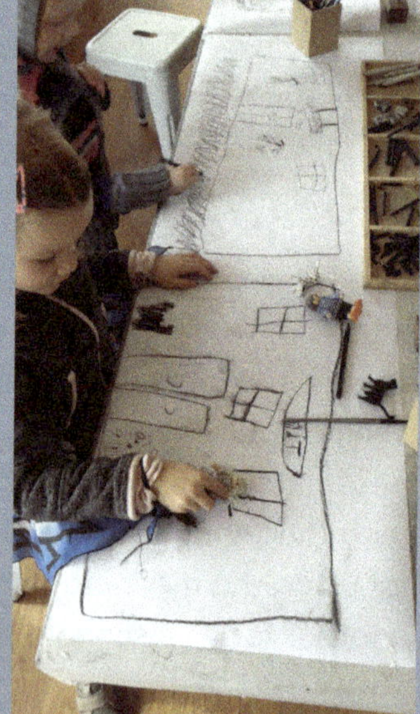

novice. If the difference between the expert and the novice is too large then there is less likelihood of transfer of skills or concepts.

When I worked with children and their drawing this was an important consideration. A peer may be more capable in one context or particular area than another. How do we decide who is the more capable? Some children are better at supporting their peers than others. Merely pairing a proficient child with one that I judge to be less adept does not guarantee that increased learning will occur.

Moll considers the issue of more capable peers in relation to local funds of knowledge. Moll used the concept to document and appreciate the many local but diverse and often essential skills and knowledge that are situated in families and communities but rarely acknowledged by teachers and schools and even more rarely actively encouraged as part of authentic classroom experiences and learning. Moll demonstrated that when local funds of knowledge are ignored or devalued then we lose a valuable source of more capable peers. Moll is suggesting our criteria for evaluating what constitutes more capable should be carefully considered (Moll 1990).

Leading activities and developmental accomplishments

This final section takes a closer look at leading activities and developmental accomplishments in the ZPD in relation to drawing. When we link drawing with leading activities, we establish a new way of looking at drawing development and the range of accomplishments involved. As children develop new accomplishments and competencies, the adults and others in their lives adjust and increase their expectations of the child.

Developmental accomplishments are the outcomes of the interaction between the child and the social context for learning. Developmental accomplishments describe new ways of thinking Vygotsky suggested that development included qualitative and quantitative changes. Qualitative changes involve a restructuring of the mind while quantitative changes involve the amount of knowledge that is accumulated. Developmental accomplishments are not components of an age/stage theory but rather a way to describe behaviors that facilitate the growth of higher mental functions at particular periods of a child's development. When the child participates in drawing activities within their ZPD and with more capable others, the child is able to move from basic random mark making to more intentional and skilled drawings. I describe in detail what some of the pedagogical strategies are in my "Manifesto for Pedagogical Practices".

Aleksei Leont'ev (Leont'ev 1977/78), a colleague of Vygotsky and a founder of activity theory, extended and elaborated on Vygotsky's idea of learning leading development. Leont'ev used the concept of leading activity to specify the types of interactions between the child and the social environment that bring about developmental accomplishments. A leading activity is the only type of interaction that will:

- produce major developmental accomplishments
- provide the basis for other activities (interactions)
- induce the creation of new mental processes and the restructuring of old ones

Children engage in many types of activities, but only the leading activity is crucial for the emergence of their next developmental accomplishment. When engaged in a leading activity, the child learns skills that make it possible to begin the transition to other types of interactions with the environment. Leading activities shape the mind in a unique way, enabling the child to generate new mental functions and to restructure current mental functions. They are the optimal activities for development (Bodrova & Leong 1996: 50).

Building on Vygotsky's theories Aleksei Leont'ev and coauthor Daniil Elkonin proposed the following leading activities:

- At the preschool stage: play, with developmental accomplishments such as imagination, symbolic functioning, integration of emotions, and thinking. This stage overlaps with the primary grade stage.
- At the primary grade stage: learning, with developmental accomplishments such as beginning of theoretical

Drawing linked with narrative can lead learning.

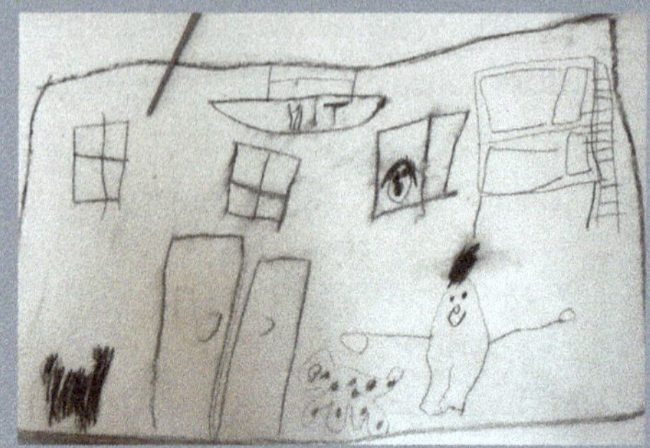

A shop that sells lollipops. There is crack in the wall because it is old (the z) The shop keeper lives there so he needs bunk beds to sleep in. The shop is closed.

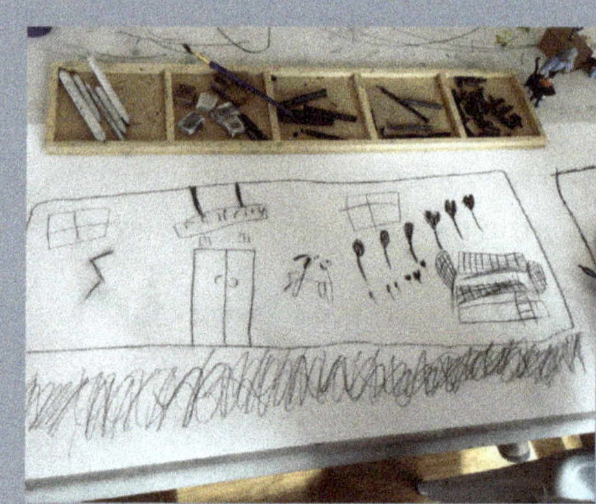

This is a pet shop selling cats and dogs. The shop keeper is tired and getting ready to go to bed in the bunk beds. The shop is closed so a customer looks in the window.

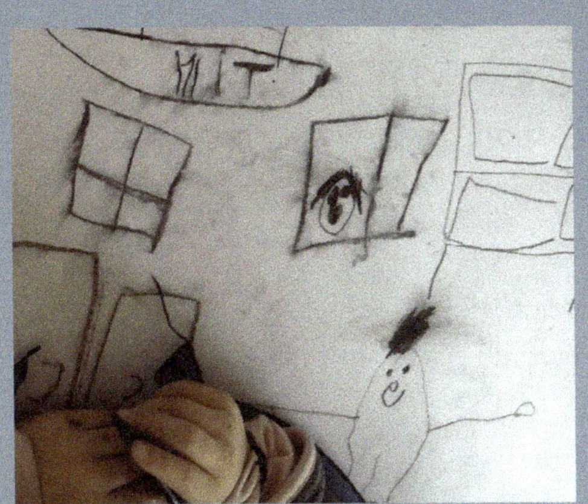

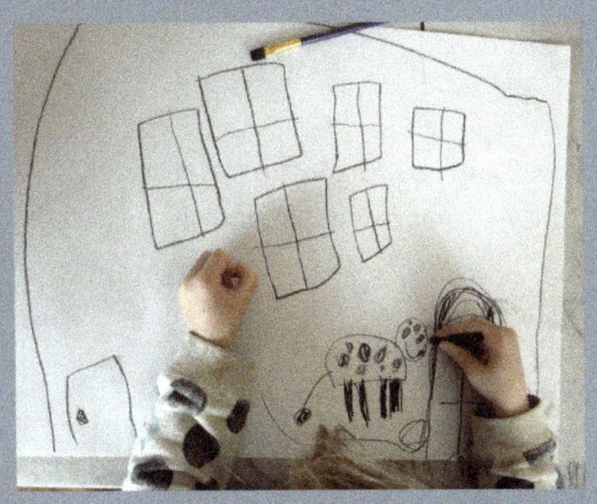

Peer scaffolding often happens through imitation. A younger child copies the idea of a pet shop. Her drawing is more elaborate than usual.

There are four key points from Vygotsky we can keep in mind in our search for ways to support the arts in young children:

1. Development cannot be separated from its social context.
2. Language plays a central role in mental development.
3. Children construct knowledge.
4. Learning can lead development.

reasoning, emergence of higher mental functions, and intrinsic motivation.

When we return to my example of Jenn and her butterflies, we can see how her process of sequencing her original drawings and redrawing her original book provide an example of major developmental accomplishment. The process of drawing led Jenn's development and induced the creation of new mental processes and the restructuring of old ones. Jenn's drawings were the leading activity that mediated between prior knowledge and the formation of new knowledge.

Play and drawing

Vygotsky considered play to be the leading activity for preschool. In play, children are acting out real-life situations in which they develop rules that move them beyond their current level of development. It is incorrect to conceive of play as activity without purpose . . . creating an imaginary situation can be regarded as a means of developing abstract thought (Vygotsky 1978: 103).

Vygotsky argues that children at play do not act in any way they please. Each role imposes its own set of rules on a child's behavior. Play mediates between thought and action. This is a very different perspective on play than the traditional Western perspective, which sees play as totally spontaneous and free of any constraints.

Elena Bodrova and Deborah Leong (1996) have written extensively about the role of play in the development of the child. They identified three particular ways in which play influences development:

1. Play creates the child's zone of proximal development.
2. Play facilitates the separation of thought from actions and objects.
3. Play facilitates the development of self-regulation.

However, for play to be considered a leading activity it needs to be robust with several interrelated roles, child-made props, and extended sequences. The scenarios used have to grow increasingly complex over time.

Play supports contexts for re-creation and an opportunity to try out different roles. When a child takes on a pretend role, they have to put themselves in place of the (typically absent) person they are representing. They have to know about and also conform to the specific set of attributes of the person or scenario they are representing. Yet they can also take a concept, story, or incident and modify it in the re-creation.

For example, three children working together to recreate a photography studio have to share their prior knowledge, assign roles, follow certain sequential procedures, and conform to the collective notion of what a photography studio should be like. Children also use drawing to facilitate a common understanding and help plan out actions and ideas. Drawing then becomes a part of the leading activity.

Drawing also facilitates the separation of thought from actions and the development of self-regulation. Some major characteristics of play that prepare children for later learning activity include symbolic representations and symbolic actions, complex interwoven themes, complex interwoven roles, and a time frame extended over several days. In play, children use objects, actions, words, and people to represent something else. This symbolic functioning paves the way for later and more complex uses of symbolic functioning like those specified in mathematics. Imagination, which is an element of play, has a generative function—it allows children to experiment with new ideas and contexts.

Drawing contains many of these elements of play and has the potential to be a leading activity, particularly if the child has to work with others in the group to explain, negotiate, and recreate. Drawing tends to be open-ended and generative. It involves the use of the imagination as well as symbolic representation. It generates the abstraction and decontextualization of specific events that are then rendered in a two-dimensional form. The child has to pull out the important points from the context and consider which ones to include in a drawing so that others will understand it. Drawings also have the flexibility of play, as the child can change or transform what they represent and how it is represented. Drawings can be done individually or collaboratively; they can be immediate responses or extend over time, becoming more complex and multilayered. They can include artefacts, techniques, and materials that are borrowed from other contexts and integrated in new ways to give different meanings.

The Photography Studio

As an extension to their study of light and shadows, the children in this early childhood class were studying the process of getting a photograph taken from beginning to end. We organized a visit to a photography studio. We started with the reception area and were shown how the receptionist makes the appointments and keeps records and details of each session. We then toured the waiting area, the prop room, the studios, the dark room, the preparation room, and the framing area. This photographer was an artist who had retained some of the traditional methods of creating photographs, like light sensitive paper and a dark room. Sometimes it is worth spending time to find the visible elements of a process. Then the child can more easily see behind the scenes and copy the sequence of events in their play.

The studio interested the children the most, especially as they were able to see several people come to get their graduation photographs taken. The children each had a clipboard with several sheets of paper so they could make many drawings and take notes about what they saw. Back in the classroom we shared the information we had gathered in our drawings and notes. This process helps build a community of learners and extend the children's knowledge about photographers.

One group of three children were very keen to recreate a photography studio in the classroom using the hollow blocks and the unit blocks. I was aware that even though these three children had experienced the same studio on their field visit they might still have very different ideas about how they could build a photography studio. I asked them each to draw a plan before they started to build. One of the challenges children face during collaborative block play is to come to a common understanding and agreement about what they will build, where it will go, and who will do the building. They often find role assignment and turn taking difficult. Everyone wants to be the photographer. If each of their ideas were made explicit through a drawing, then we would have a vehicle whereby we might more easily reach a common understanding.

One child began building without looking at the others' drawings and ideas first. This created a heated discussion. Eventually a process of negotiation evolved whereby the children recalled and shared important information through the drawings they had done in the studio. One child remembered that when he took a picture of someone who was too close to the camera then the picture was "all foggy." Using their drawings as mediating tools they negotiated a suitable distance between the seat and the camera as well as how high the camera should be. One child drew a person to show the camera in proportional relation to a child.

From their drawings it became clear that there was a significant difference between two children's understanding of the scale

Drawing plans for a photography studio

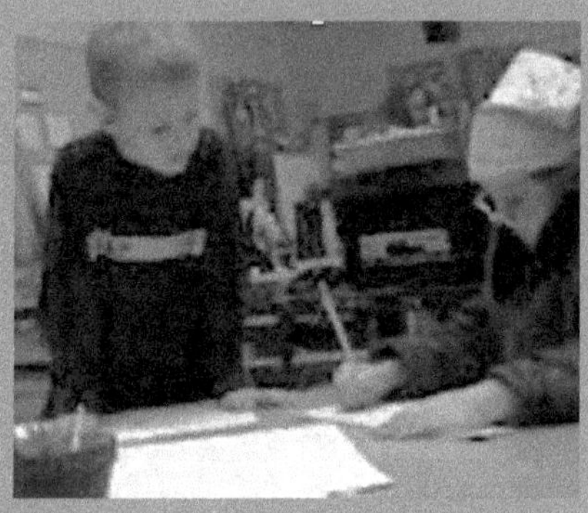

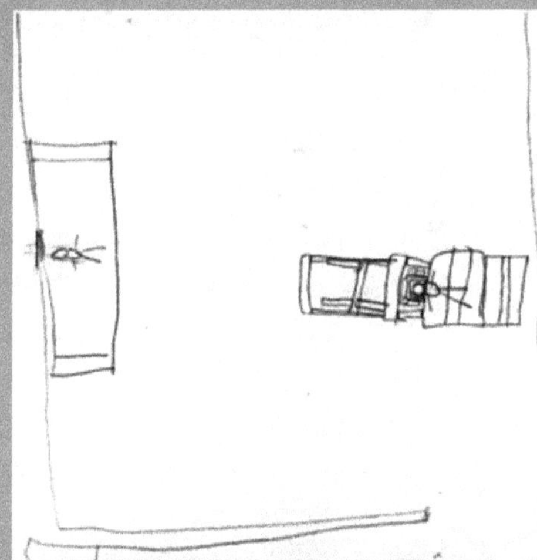

The client is sitting on the sofa on the left and on the right is the camera.

of the project. One child assumed they were going to use only the unit blocks while another child assumed they were going to use the larger hollow blocks. Sharing their drawings clarified this point while also helping resolve it. Anton re-evaluated his drawing and labeled it with the words "holo block."

From this discussion and the drawings we can see how each child had many ideas. However, in the excitement of building, not all ideas were easily heard or recognized. Drawing not only slowed the process down and made the children more thoughtful, it also helped to make their ideas visible and easier to understand.

The children also used their drawings to assist other children in becoming meaningful participants in their play event. They showed their drawings to Susan and she was quickly able to see that they did not yet have a developing studio. She was able to negotiate her entry into their play by producing a drawing of a processing department and explaining her idea and the role she would play. Using drawing as an entry device to a play event alleviated the typical rejection that comes with the more ambiguous question, "Can I play?"

After the children built the studio they assigned roles and began the process of taking photographs and processing them. One child sat on the client's seat while the other looked through the "camera lens" and drew a simple line drawing of the seated person. Next, the photographer took the simple drawing to the processing room. To represent what happened when a photograph was processed, the children in the processing room shaded the line drawings different shades of grey. The finished product was then "sold" to the client.

Using drawings as a mediating tool within the social context of block play proves to be a successful tool for self-regulation. Drawing helps mediate between thought and action. The children did not all begin building in the random and impulsive manner that often leads to disagreement and the breakdown of the play sequence. Drawing helped the children clarify their thinking and share it with others. The process of drawing aided memory and the children remembered many particulars from their field visit. Drawing helped the children come to a common understanding about how the play event would be constructed and what their various roles might be. As they discussed their drawings they could easily see different understandings that needed to be clarified before they started building. I see play and drawing working together to lead development. Drawing in the context of play and project work has proven extremely effective in directing children's attention and lifting play to a more productive level. With the aid of drawing, play can become complex with multiple roles, sequences of events, and sustained activity over several days. In other words, play reaches a level at which it can be classified as a leading activity.

Drawing can assist self regulation by slowing down the action and helping children come to a common understanding and game plan. However, play suffers from the same pedagogical neglect as art. Children are left to play without adult input. In my visits to centers I often see stereotypical play where the same roles are played over and again and the setting is rarely changed or enhanced. Play in this instance becomes superficial and short term with few complex roles and events. Children wander in and out of play each time causing aninterruption in the flow of play. This kind of play does not lead development; it becomes another superficial activity and a way to fill time. Like drawing and art, play needs the guidance of a knowledgeable adult.

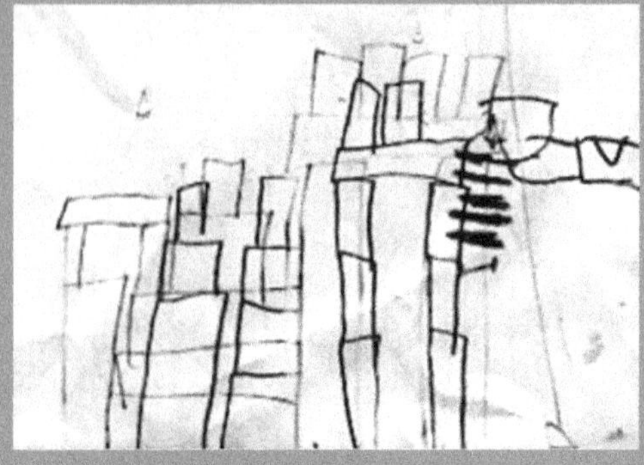

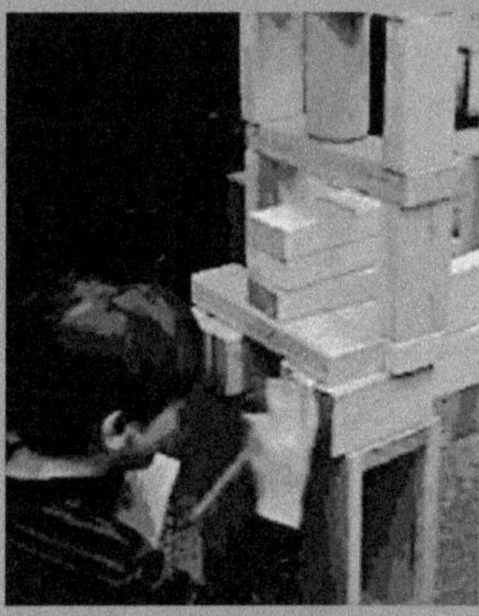

This child used unit blocks and hollow blocks to construct the camera

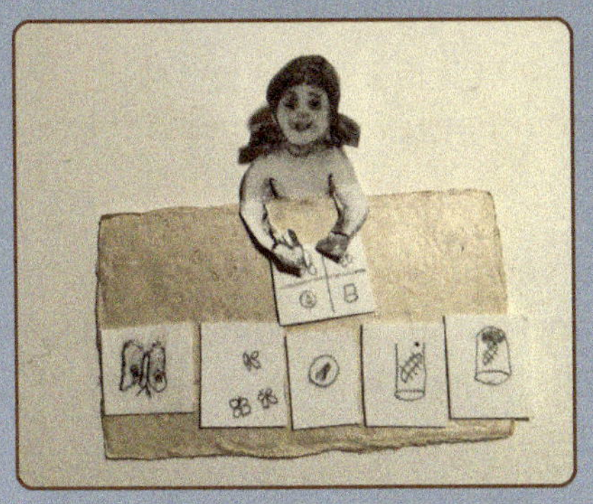

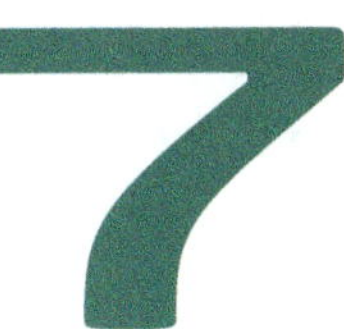

7

Imagination and Creativity

It has puzzled me that teachers of arts in early childhood have not paid more attention to the work of Vygotsky. We tend to forget that Vygotsky began his career with the psychology of art. He has written about the arts, imagination, and creativity, but his theories in this domain have not really made their way into art and early childhood. Some theories in his psychology of the arts are worth thinking more about in relation to the arts and young children.

Vygotsky outlines his theories about imagination and creativity in childhood in an article. He defines creativity as:

> *Any human act that gives rise to something new is referred to as a creative act, regardless of whether what is created is a physical object or some mental or emotional construct that lives within the person who created it and is known only to him. (Vygotsky 2004)*

He makes it clear that creativity is not just the domain of geniuses but something we can all do. Whenever we imagine or combine or alter something to create something new we are involved in a creative act.

In early childhood, imagination and creativity can most easily be observed in play. When a child uses a stick to represent a horse; when a child pretends to be the doll's grandmother; when another leaps into a car made from blocks and drives to the repair shop; these are all demonstrations of creative and imaginative thinking. When children play, they do not just reproduce exactly what they have experienced but rather they draw from their experiences to recreate a new reality, one that fits with their desires and needs. Imagination and creativity can also be seen when children draw and make up stories. The child's ability to take elements from the environment and his or her experiences and use their imagination to make something new is the foundation of their creativity.

To better understand what underpins imagination, Vygotsky suggests that we need to look more carefully at the relationship between fantasy and reality. He lists four basic ways that imagination is associated with reality.

The first type of association establishes that everything the child imagines is based on previous experiences. Their imagination is built on objects and incidents from reality. A child's experiences are the food for his or her imagination. The richer they are, the better fed is the imagination. Imagination therefore depends on the quality, richness, and breadth of the experiences encountered. An experience does not necessarily have to be exotic. For example, think about an everyday event like a child's trip to the supermarket. One child's family includes the child in preparing to go shopping by checking the cupboards and writing a list together. At the supermarket, the child takes part of the list and a small shopping cart and is supported in navigating the store and finding the items on the list. The child helps check out the groceries and pay for them. Compare this experience with the busy parent who plops the child in the shopping cart and races around the supermarket while telling the child not to touch anything. The first child had a rich experience, because of this, their imagination will have much more to draw upon when playing shopping.

The implication for teachers' planning and programming is that in order to support imagination and creativity we need to make sure that the child is exposed to a wide range of multisensory, rich experiences. The more in-depth and meaningful they are, the more the child will have to draw upon. The richer the experiences we can provide, the richer the imagination will be.

The second type of association is based on second-hand information. A child's imagination is not confined to immediate and real experiences but also includes things the child has heard, viewed, and read. The child extends his or her imagination by taking in things from another's rendition, representation, or narration, so that information from books, videos, and exhibitions also becomes a pool of experience the child can access. There is a mutual dependence between imagination and experiences of all kinds. However, for young children, second-hand information is not as satisfactory as first hand involvement. With second-hand information there is a danger that the child's knowledge can be at a level of recitation with little deep understanding. Children can often talk about things using all the right vocabulary even as they have no real understanding. For young children, the priority must be rich, multimodal, first-hand participation.

The third type of association between imagination and reality is an emotional one. Images and objects contain affect, which is to say they arouse certain feelings. We make connections between images that arouse the same or a similar affect. They can then be grouped together even though they might be quite different objectively. Making connections at an emotional level yields very different results than simply observing dispassionately. Groupings that arise from emotions will be different from the those that arise from experience. When first-hand and second-hand experiences and emotion bind together, they create both internal and external truth.

The fourth type of association concerns fantasy. Fantasy is something unknown and completely new that has no direct links to reality. It is a link between a child's imagination and a reality that exists solely within that imagination.

In the context of school and formal education, emotion and fantasy are often neglected. Yet it is these elements and associations that are most powerful and memorable for the child. Think about how an imaginative narrative can hold a child's attention or a work of art can engage at an emotional level. If we want to promote imagination and creativity, it is necessary that we as educators address expressions of emotion and fantasy. Together these four associations demonstrate the multiple connections that can occur in the creation of something new and unique.

Vygotsky also talks about the process of creation. He acknowledges that it is difficult to see this process. Creation is a process that builds upon itself and depends on an accumulation of rich experiences and materials. The child takes experiences and feelings and collects material that they will use to construct something new. The process is a cyclical and recurring one that reworks the materials with mindful deconstruction and reconstruction. It is this progression that feeds the imagination and seems to come naturally to children. They are very motivated to play with art materials, loose parts, blocks, and open-ended construction toys and will create endless combinations. They take apart bits of machinery like old record players and repurpose the parts to fulfill outcomes created by their imagination. Things are taken apart and reassembled in new ways. Their drawings usually contain a combination of reality and fantasy. In the classroom, we must provide a good supply of open-ended materials together with spaces and support for the deconstruction and reconstruction of that material.

A Project about Sunflowers

If rich experiences are important for the development of imagination and creativity, what is a "rich experience" and where does art fit in? We don't necessarily have to provide exotic excursions nor do we need a lot of expensive equipment. We do need to plan for extensive investigation over extended periods of time and develop communities of learners in which children share ideas so that the collective knowledge builds upon itself. Much depends on the teacher's ability to listen carefully to what children are saying, discover what they are thinking, explore their big ideas, and be responsive. Much also depends on the teacher's ability to be creative.

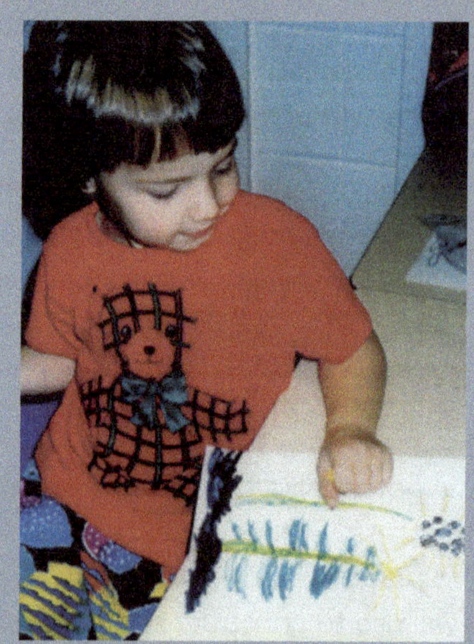

As an example of a simple yet deep experience that is meaningful for the child I will share bits of a project about sunflowers that I did during the first month in kindergarten with a group of children aged three to six. On my home visits before kindergarten started I had noticed that nearly all the

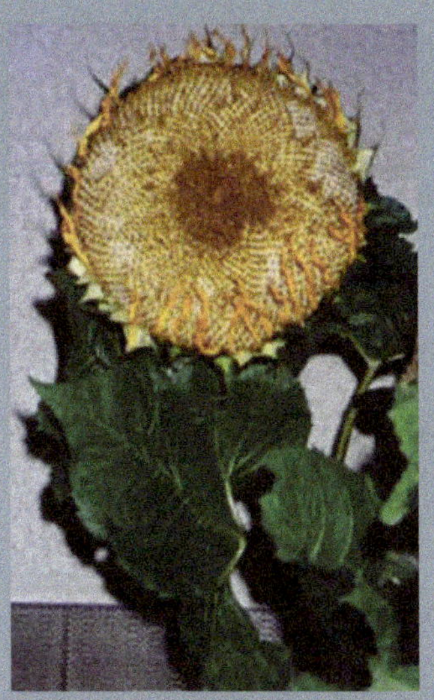

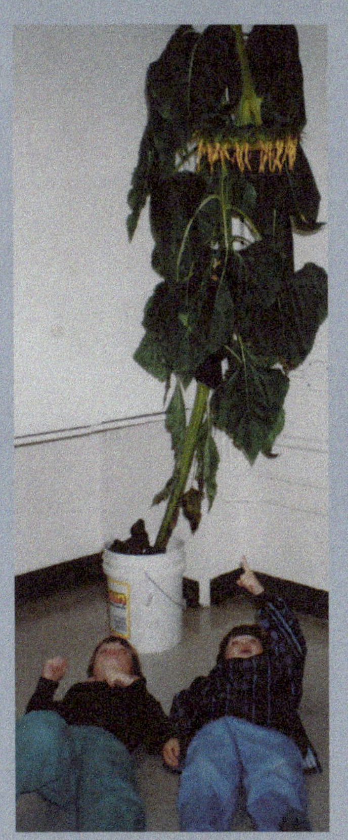

children had grown sunflowers in their gardens over summer. This meant sunflowers and gardening was a familiar topic and the children would have many experiences to share. For example, one family had planted a circle of seeds and they had grown up to form an enclosed space—a sunflower tent—where I had morning tea on my visit. Another child's sunflower was growing wild in the gutter of his house.

On the first day of kindergarten on one table I made a simple display of photos, drawings, and paintings of sunflowers along with paper and art materials for the children to represent their memories of sunflowers. This was a conscious effort to establish links between home and school. Heather immediately drew her sunflower tent, happy to draw a memory from home.

Later that week Heather's parents dug up one of the sunflowers and brought it, roots and all, into the kindergarten. It was too big and heavy to stand by itself so we hung it from the ceiling in a corner of the room.

The children gathered around it and examined it carefully. Two boys lay down under the huge flower head to see it more clearly. They were discussing the number of seeds and the size of the plant. It was ten times his size, said James. Another child found a lady beetle. The sunflower provided a context for children to share their own knowledge of sunflowers. At large group time, the children shared their personal stories about sunflowers and we compiled a list of children's questions. We were laying the groundwork to begin in-depth investigations in a project approach.

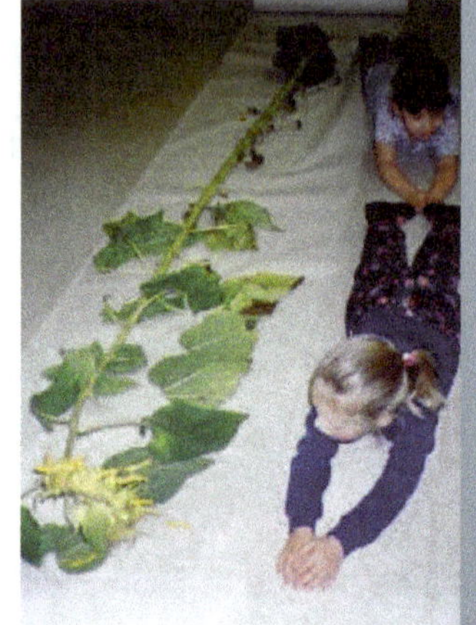

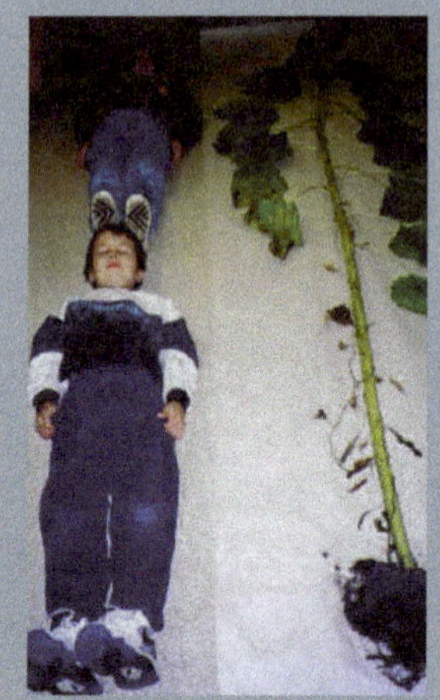

Heather's parents brought in another sunflower, and this time we laid it down on the floor. The two girls immediately lay down beside it to see how tall it was. If they stretched out it was as tall as two girls.

The boys thought they were taller than the girls and would not need to stretch out. They said it was exactly two whole boys tall.

But Anna, who had been watching, insisted they only came as far as the flower head. She lay down and added her head size to their height to show that the plant was two boys and one head tall.

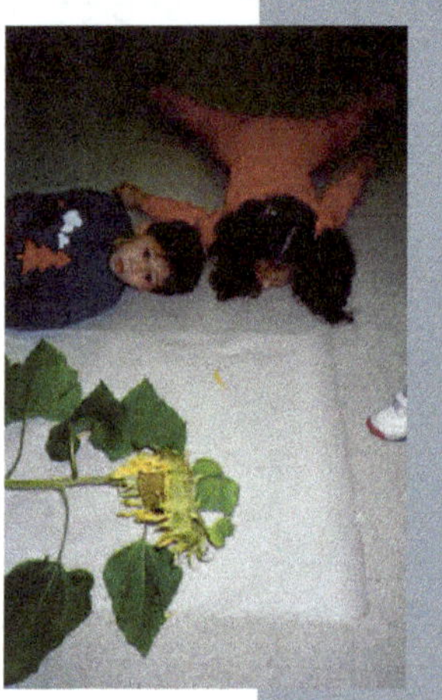

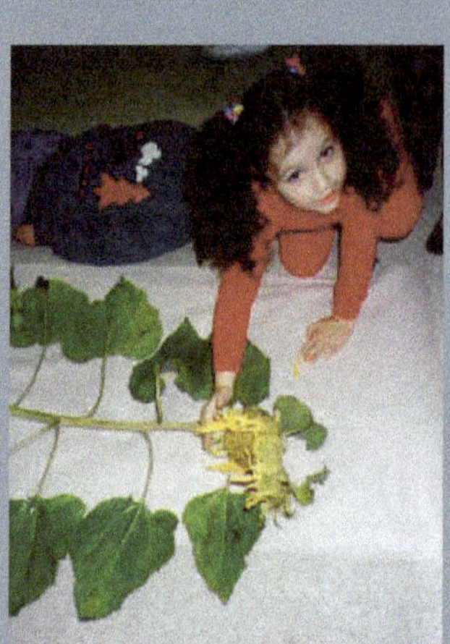

The three boys were able to take a closer look now that the flower was down on the floor. They felt the weight of the seed head and examined the seeds. They wanted to draw it so I rolled another length of paper out beside the flower and gave them some vine charcoal. They took turns to draw and offer each other advice. The scale of the flower made it quite a challenging exercise for them. They were keen to have their drawing match the size of the plant.

Max drew the leaves. He drew them without looking at the plant. His leaves were small and covered all of the stem. He drew many more leaves than there were and he drew the leaves quite a different shape. Next he helped his friend try to draw all the seeds in the flower head. They wondered how many seeds there really were.

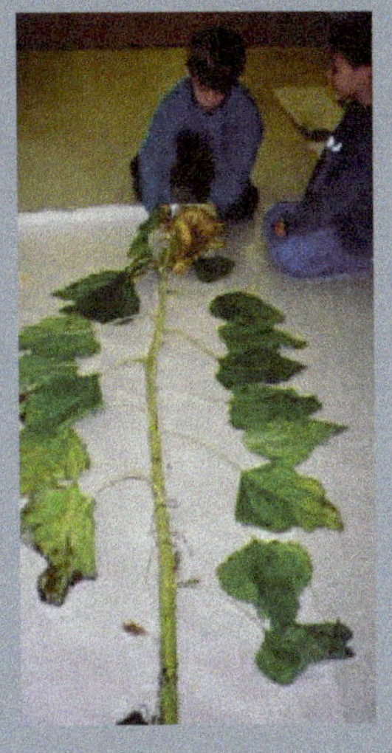

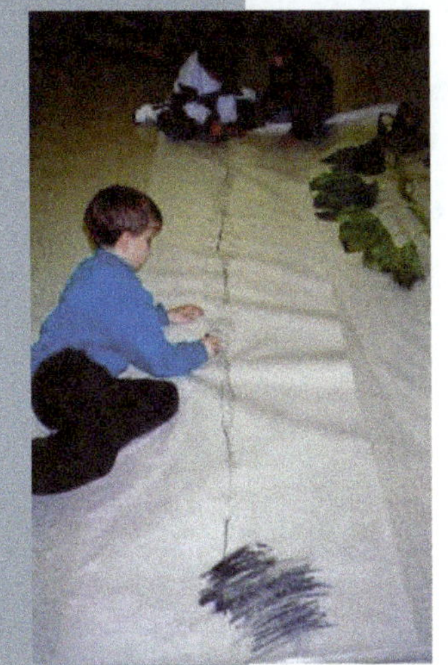

The three boys invited me to look at their drawing. They had never done something so big before and they were worried they had missed something. The main problem they had drawing was that they were drawing what they knew rather than what they saw. Max had drawn the bulk of the root ball but had not drawn the roots.

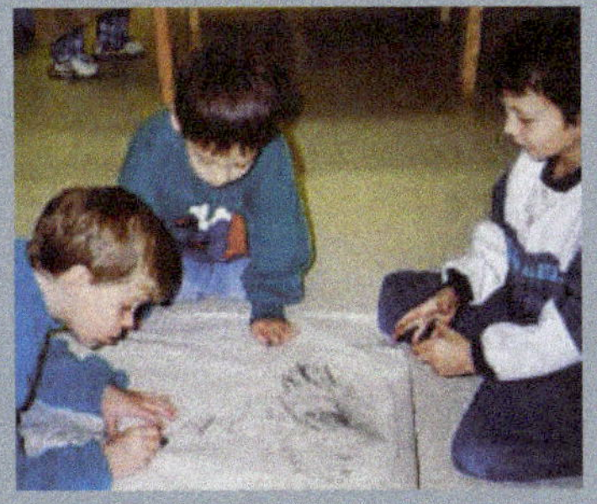

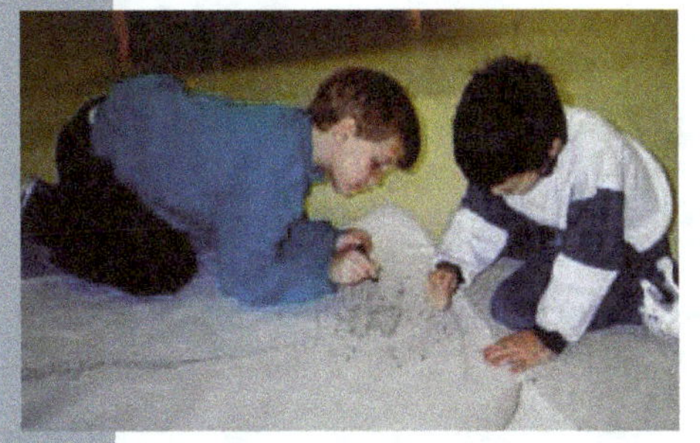

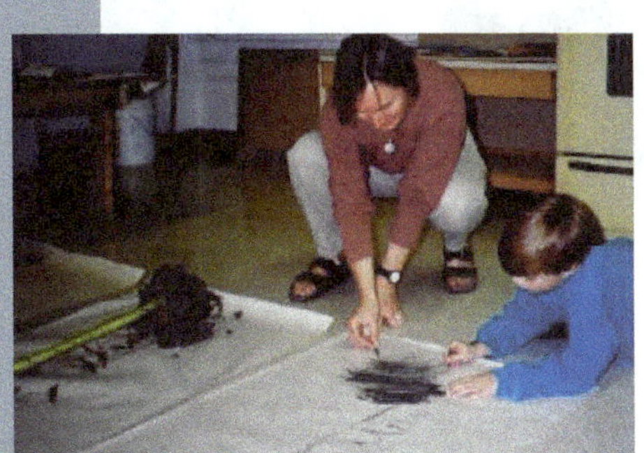

Anna had been watching the three boys draw, and when they finished she asked if she could try. Anna had overheard my conversations about the leaves and roots in the root ball, and she very studiously recorded as many roots as she could. Next, she tackled the leaves. She had a special plan for drawing them so they were in the right place and the right size and number. First, she counted the leaves on each side of the stem. Then beginning at one end of the stalk she carefully lifted the leaf she was going to draw and had a good look at it. When she put it down she carefully slid backwards in line with the leaf and drew it exactly where she stopped. Having had a good look at each leaf, her drawing was more congruent with the flower's actual shape and size. She spent a long time drawing each seed in the flower head.

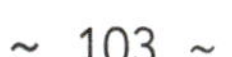

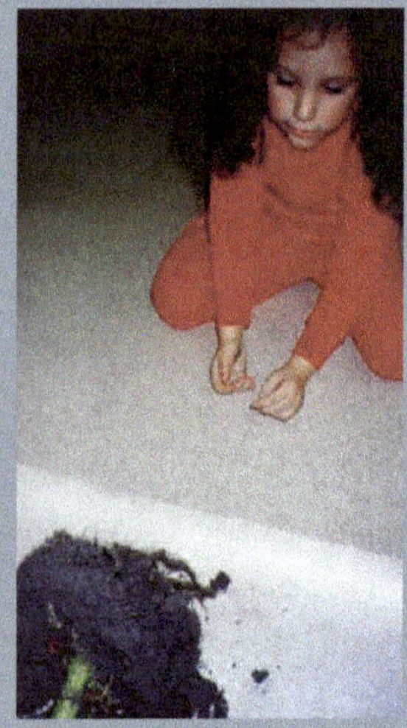
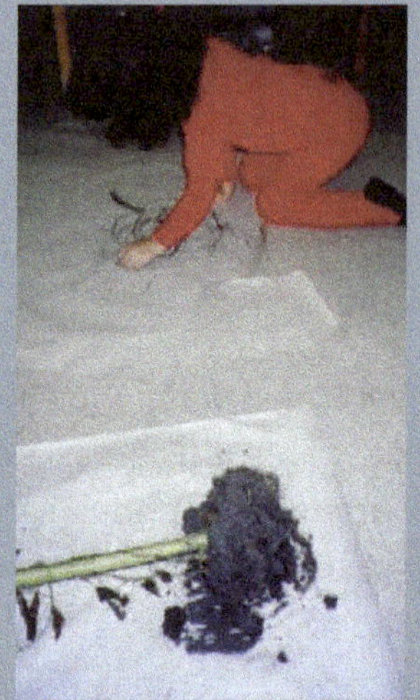
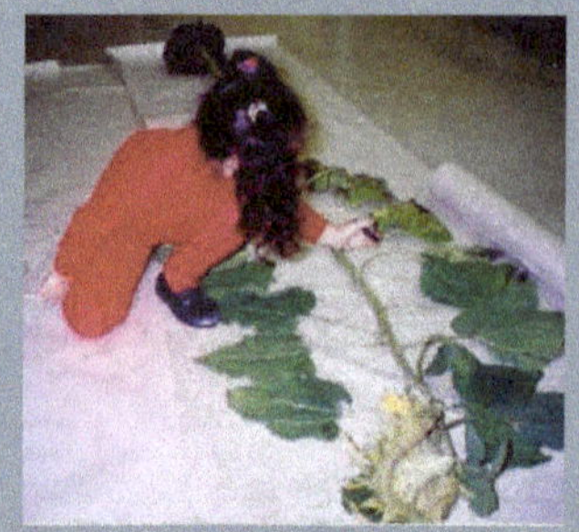
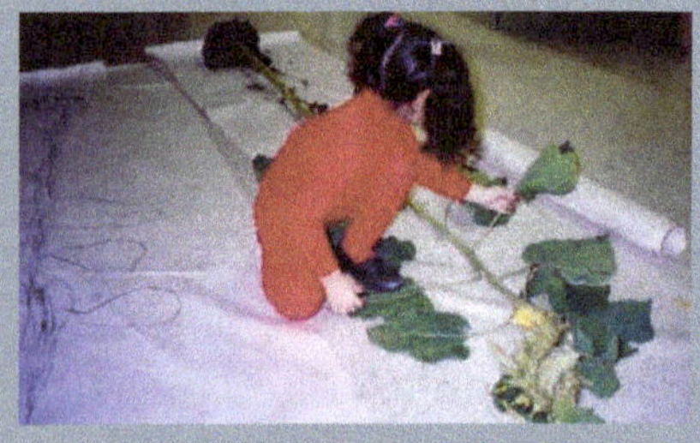
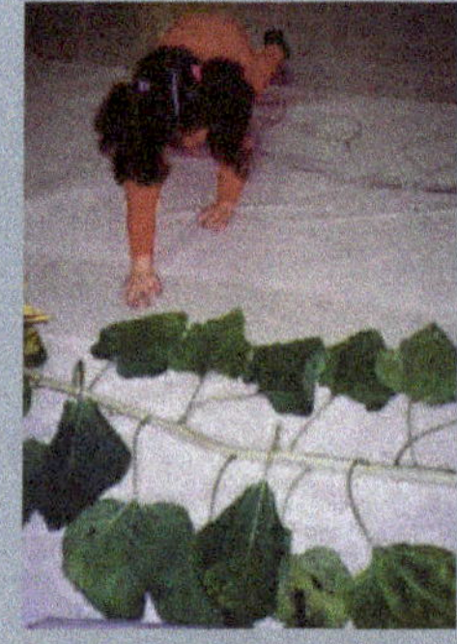
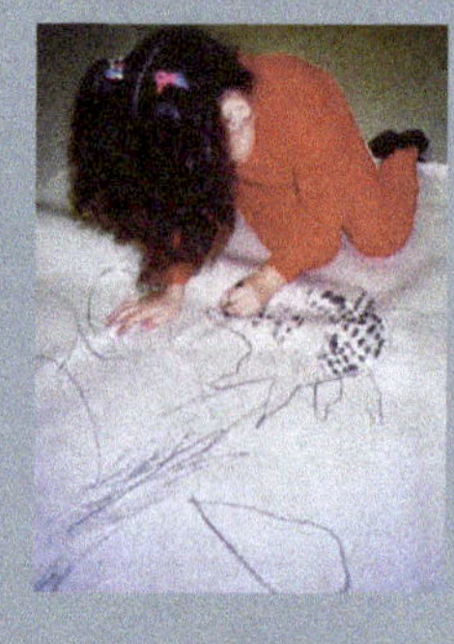
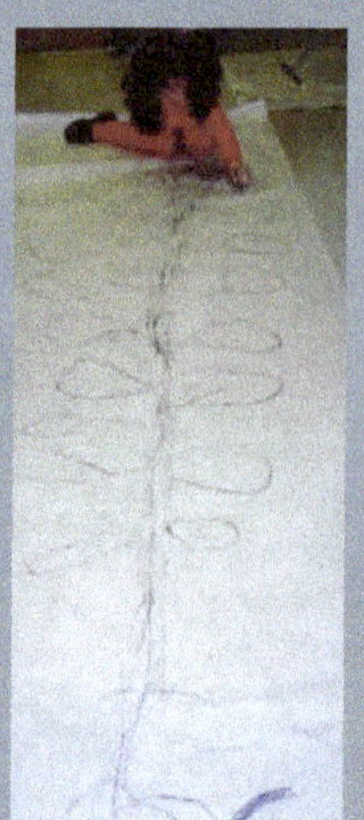

Anna drawing the sunflower. First she looks hard at the root ball, then she draws the root ball. Then she counts the leaves, checks how many by touching each one, measures by crawling backward from each leaf until she has drawn all the leaves. Then she carefully draws the seeds.

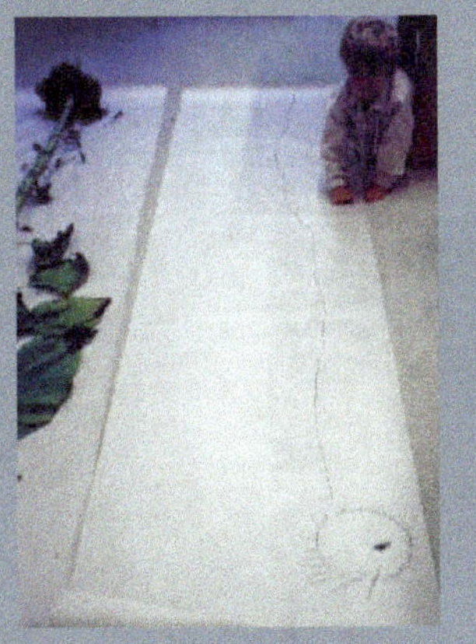

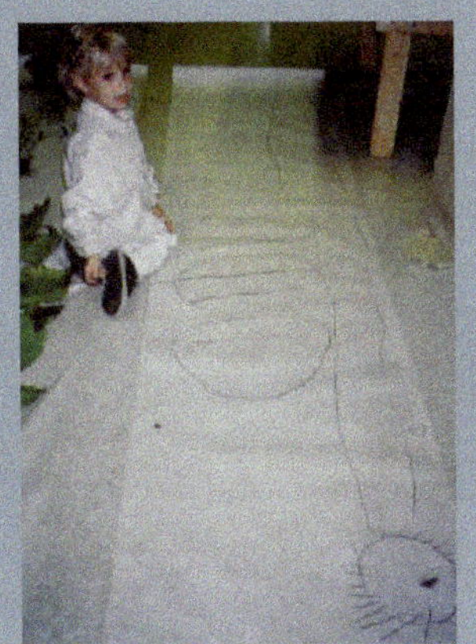

Already we can see the consequential progression of ideas. We can also see thinking and drawing coming together to create meaning. Anna's knowledge and understanding of sunflowers is already considerably greater than before. Her imagination has propelled her forward to create her own unique version of the sunflower. Within this rich experience she is gaining a deeper understanding of the components of this flower. She has gone through the process of deconstruction and reconstruction to construct her very own creation.

Three-year-old Michael insisted that he too could draw the sunflower. He worked independently, beginning at the flower head, and drew one of each of the essential elements he had learned from class discussions: the petal, the seed, the stem, the root, and a leaf. He was very proud of his accomplishment. Michael's drawing is a wonderful example of learning leading development. While he is not yet able to make a more elaborate drawing, he has managed to draw the key elements of the flower. In this mixed-age class the children support each other. From watching more capable others he has gathered enough information and confidence to want to try for himself. One could say here that Michael was working in the upper end of his ZPD with his classmates providing the scaffolding he needed.

Next Heather and Ann confidently launch into a much more detailed drawing of the flower. They begin at either end. Ann quickly completes the root ball and comes to help draw all the seeds. The girls notice the stalk has lots of hairs so they are drawn along with good sized leaves. They also notice that the leaves have veins and wonder how they work.

A series of 4 images that show two girls working together to draw the sunflower. They begin with one at each end then work together to draw the bristles on the stem. Two images of them working on the seed head.

I hung the four drawings on the walls behind the sunflower as a reference point. Carefully displaying children's work with documentation about the process allows others to see the thinking behind the work. Those who are drawing can take inspiration from the display. The documentation combined with our class meetings together create a community of learners. A community of learners provides a rich bank of wonderings, questions, experiences, discoveries, and solutions that all the members of the group have access to. Being a part of a community of learners provides more opportunities for creative connections than working in independent isolation.

Charcoal was not the only media children used for this project. Elsewhere, in collaboration with the children, I provided different media and spaces for the children to have different experiences and to try new representations. Some children made sunflowers with clay. A group of children set up a stall in the hollow block area and role played selling sunflower seeds and oil. Another small group sold dried and packaged seeds as snacks in the

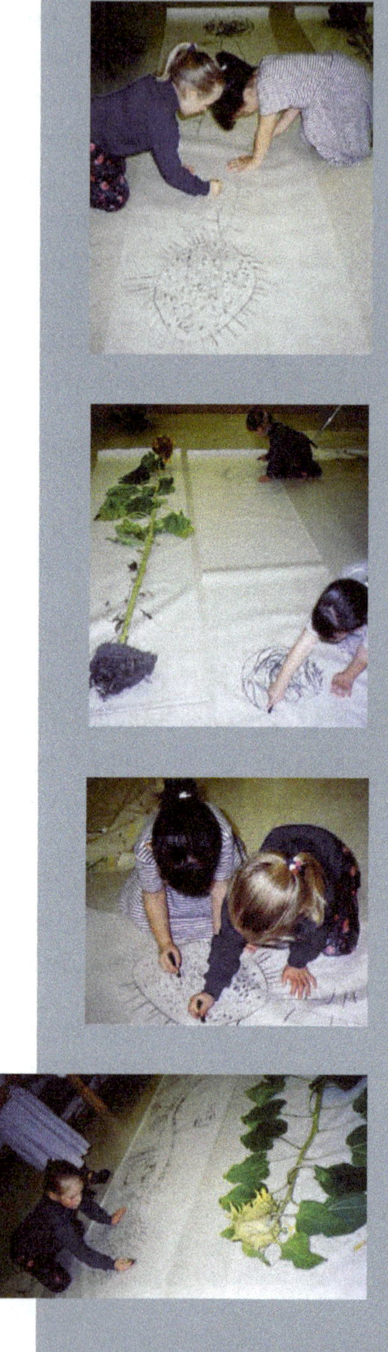

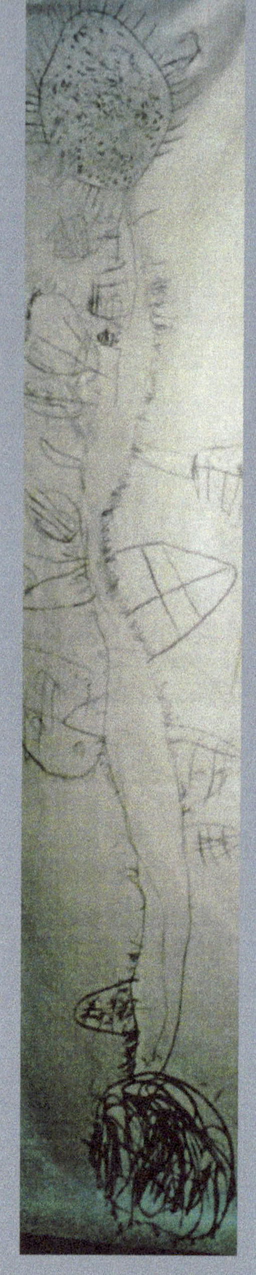

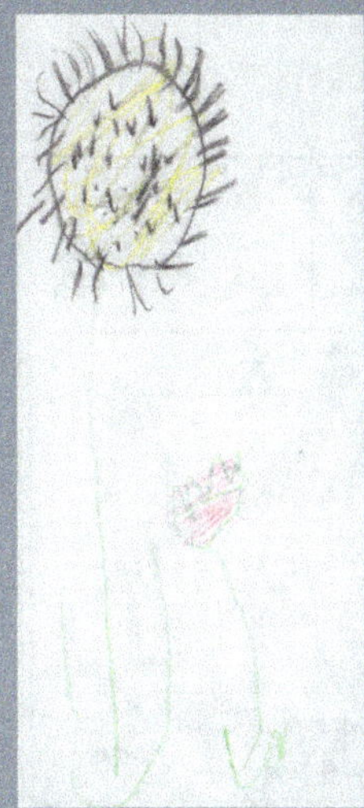
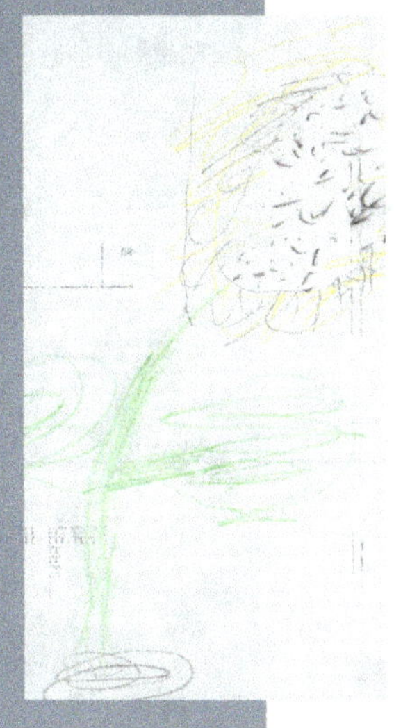
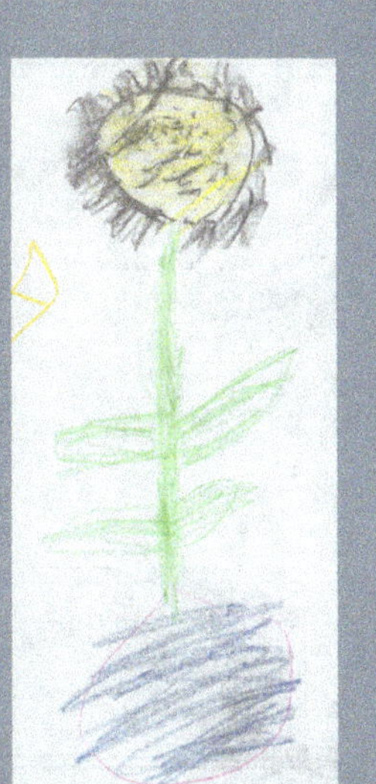
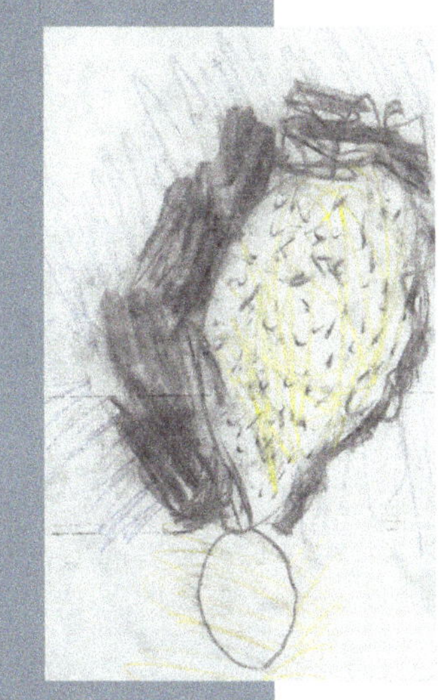

play shop. One small group worked with a parent to try to crush the seeds to try to get oil and to do some baking with the seeds. Yet another group planted seeds and soon had small seedlings to observe, draw, and care for. Eventually they created a plant shop and sold the seedlings. Some children enjoyed creating sunflower heads from pattern blocks. Others sorted and counted a pile of seeds on the math table. All of these activities were in response to the children's questions and interests.

Finally, I invited my artist friend, Tanya, in to the class room to draw sunflowers. At this time, I also set up a small art studio where a few children could work beside Tanya. She arranged the sunflowers and made several charcoal drawings of them. The children watched and then worked beside her on their own interpretations. The artist was acting as a mentor who understood that children would pick and choose from the techniques she was modelling as they needed.

Out of all these different experiences came some wonderful artwork. One of my favorite examples was when, unprompted by me, Ann presented me with four drawings she had done.

"Look," she said, "We have done SO much work on sunflowers." She explained her drawings. "First, we have sunflowers in our gardens with other flowers, and then Heather brought in a big one and hung it up. This is when the sunflower was lying down and we drew it and last is beautiful drawings we made with Tanya." Here is another example similar to Jenn's sequence of events. Ann has compiled her learning journey and realized she is now quite an expert on sunflowers. I asked her where her idea of making these drawings came from and she told me that she noticed that I always told stories about their work on the wall displays. This was her story, a wonderful example of drawing, thinking, and meaning making.

Below are just a few of the other drawings the children did. Each brought their own creative interpretation to their drawings. We hung them on an impromptu gallery wall where they were much admired by families and visitors.

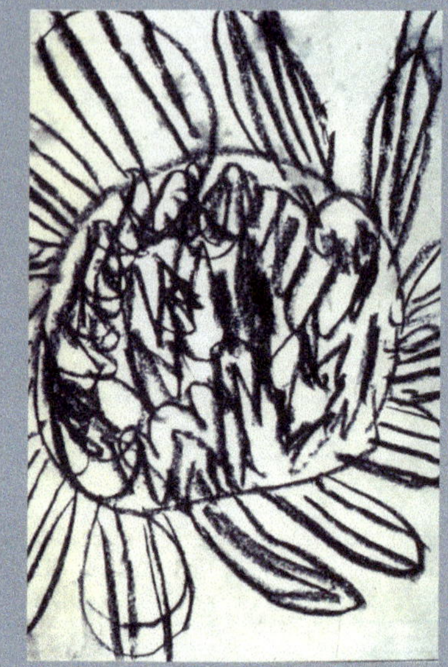

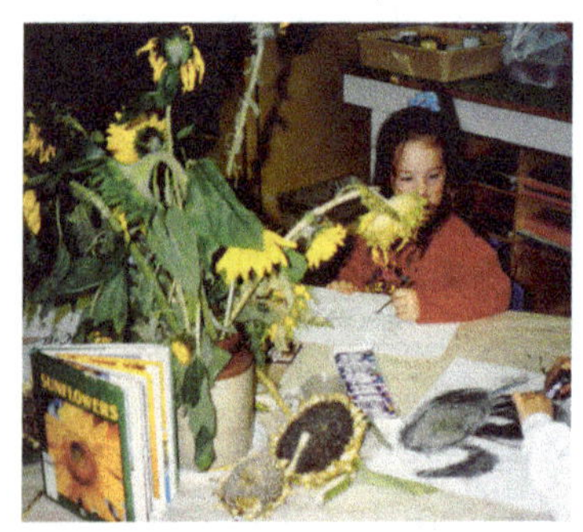

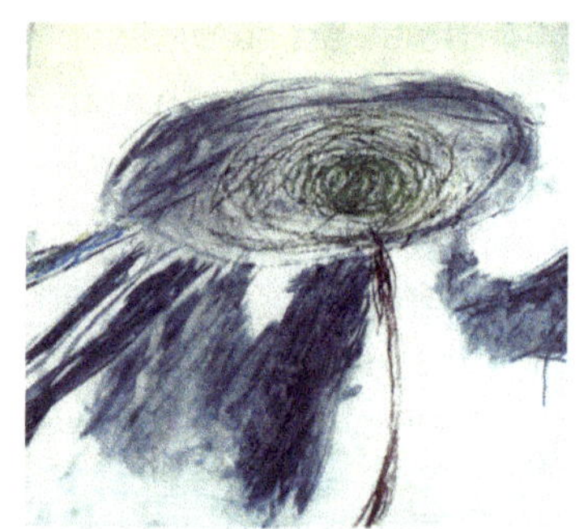

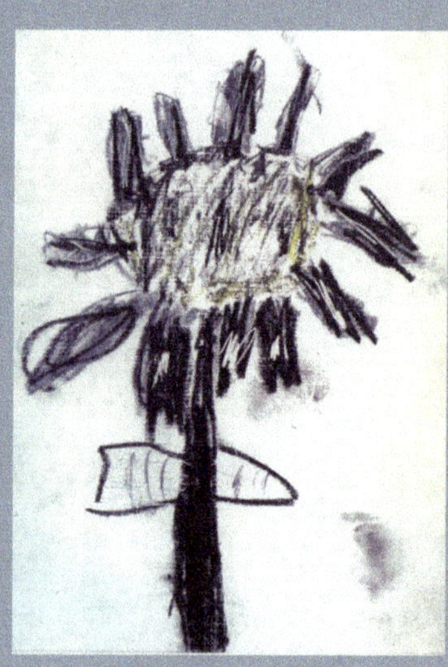

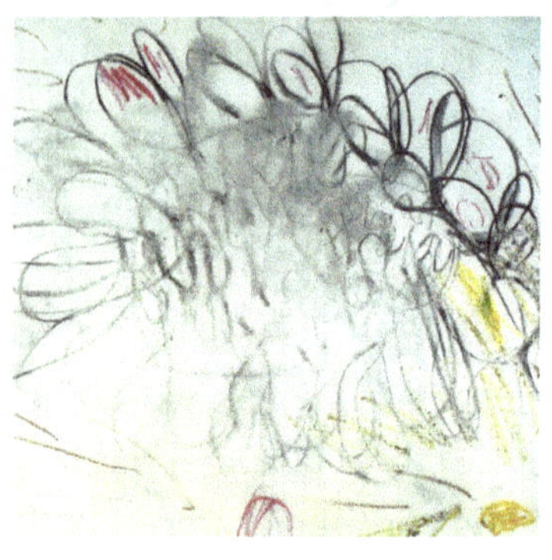

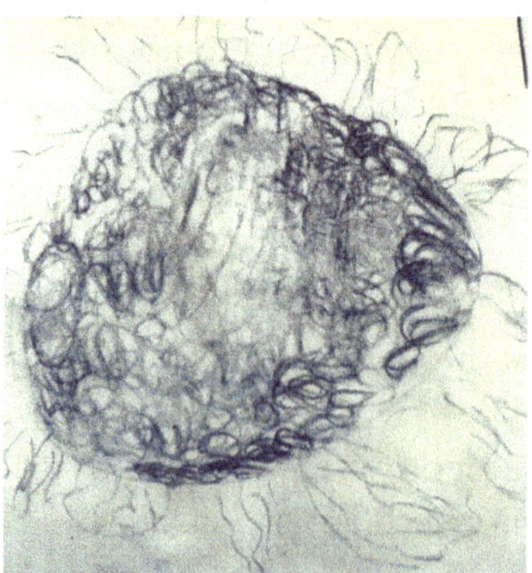

In this short description of a sunflower project I have identified the many ways Vygotsky's theories are supporting learning. Marrying the arts to Vygotsky seems to me to be a productive way of analysing and validating the work children do with the arts. For more Vygotskian theory please see the companion book to this, 'Authentic Art'.

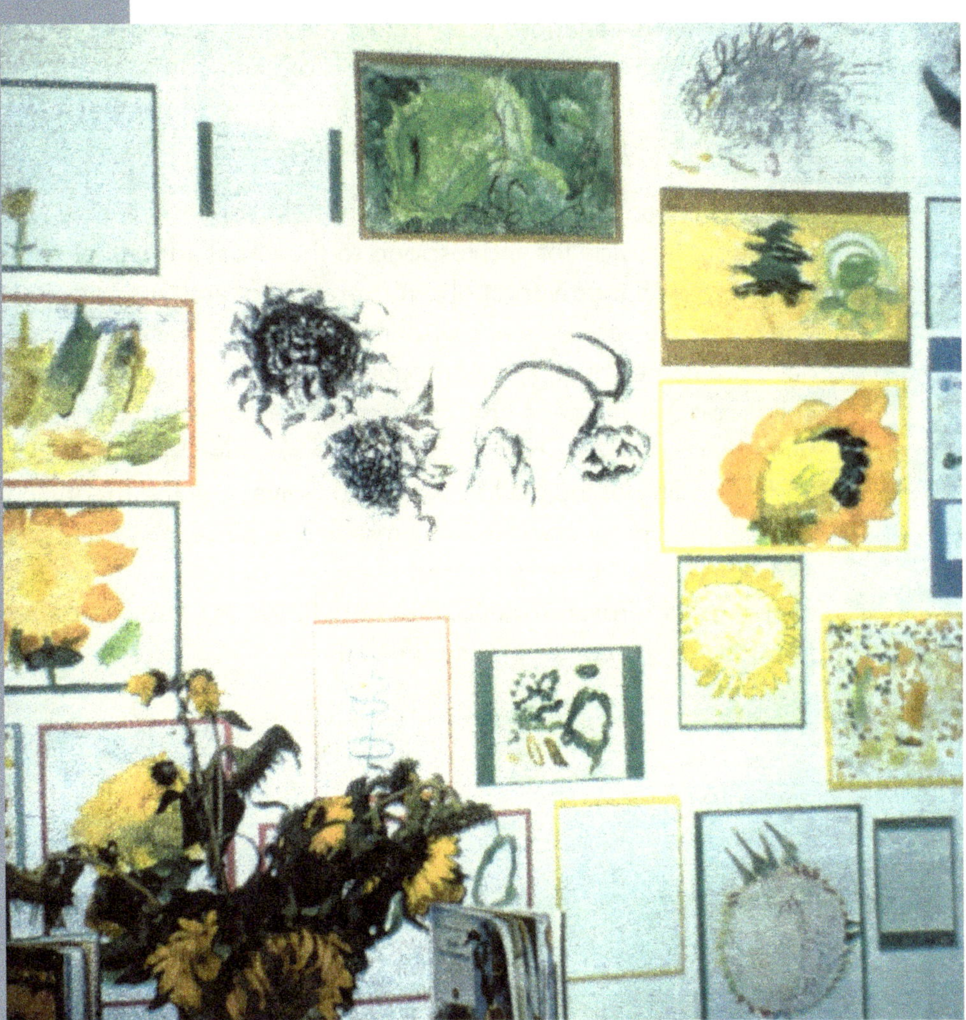

Their drawings displayed on the 'gallery wall' behind a pot of sunflowers

Conclusion

One's approach to pedagogy is underpinned by a strong theoretical framework. When we have a clear understanding about why we teach the way we do, we can more easily select the most appropriate approach. This book has tried to demonstrate what art projects with a strong Vygotskian, socio cultural underpinning look like and the potential they have for extending children's thinking and learning.

I hope this book has been a catalyst to help you rethink how we engage, talk about, provide for and respond to the visual arts with young children. I have threaded theory throughout examples of authentic art projects so that you can more easily see and understand the relevance and importance of having a framework that is compatible with contemporary theories in early childhood. Having seen how children can engage with big ideas through the arts, you will now be able to provide experiences that extend children's understanding of the world in which they live. Use the theory in this book as a guide for a more appropriately responsive pedagogy in the visual arts in early childhood I have described the many roles an adult can have that will support children's art making. Please build on this knowledge and these skills to put art at the center of the curriculum.

References

Arden, R., Garfield, V., Plomin, R., Trzaskowski, M., (2014) Genes Influence Young Children's Human Figure Drawings and Their Association With Intelligence a Decade Later. Psychological Science, Sage Journals.

Arnheim, R. (1969). Visual thinking. Berkeley: University of California Press.

Arnheim, R. (1974). Art and visual perception: A psychology of the creative eye. The new version. Berkley and Los Angeles: University of California Press.

Bodrova, E., Leong, D.J. (1996). Tools of the mind - The Vygotskian approach to early childhood education. Columbus, Ohio: Merrill/Prentice Hall.

Bruner, J. (1983). Vygotsky's zone of proximal development: The hidden agenda. New Directions for Child Development, 23, 93-97.

Bruner, J. (1986). Actual minds, possible worlds. Cambridge: Harvard University Press.

Cazden, C, B. (2017) Communicative competence, classroom interaction, and educational equity: The selected works of Courtney B. Cazden. Routledge, New York.

Charman, H. & Ross, M., 2004. 'Contemporary Art and the Role of Interpretation', Tate Papers No. 2.

Cole, M., Gay, J., Glick, J., Sharp, D. (1971) The cultural context of learning and thinking: An exploration in experimental anthropology. New York: Basic Books.

Colwell J, Pollard A (Ed) (2015). Readings for Reflective Teaching in Early Education. Bloomsbury Publishing, London

Costall, A. (1993). Conflicting images of innocence and corruption in the valuation of child art. In, A.M. Kindler, (Ed). (1997) Child Development in art. Reston, Virginia: National Art Foundation.

Cox, M. V. (1991). The child's point of view. (2nd Ed.) London: Harvester Wheatsheaf Cox, M. V.

(1993). Children's drawings of the human figure. Hove: UK: Erlbaum.

Darras, B. & Kindler, A. M. (1997) Map of artistic development. In A.M. Kindler, (Ed). (1997) Child Development in art. Reston, Virginia: National Art Foundation.

Davis, J. (1997). The 'u' and the wheel of 'C': Development and devaluation of graphic symbolization and the cognitive approach at Harvard project zero. In Kindler, A. M., (Ed.). (1997) Child Development in Art. Reston, Virginia: National Art Foundation.

Edwards, C., Gandini, L., Forman, G.,(2011) The Hundred Languages of Children: The Reggio Emilia Experience in Transformation. Praeger.

Eisner, E, W. (2002). The Arts and the Creation of Mind. Yale University Press.

Fernandes, M. A., Wammes, J. D., Meade, M. E.,

'The Surprisingly Powerful Influence of Drawing on Memory', 2018. Sage Journals, https://doi.org/10.1177/0963721418755385

Freedman, K. (1997). Artistic development and curriculum: Sociocultural learning considerations. In, A. M. Kindler, (Ed.). (1997) Child Development in Art. Reston, Virginia: National Art Foundation.

Freeman, N. H. (1980). Strategies of representation in young children: Analysis of spatial skills and drawing processes. London: Academic Press Inc.

Gardner, H., (2011) Frames of mind: The theory of multiple intelligences. Hachette, UK Gilbert, J. (2005). Visualization in Science Education. Springer.

Golomb, C. (1989). The child's creation of a pictorial world: Studies in the psychology of art. Berkeley, CA: University of California Press.

Goodenough, F. (1926). Draw a figure test. Retrieved https://depts.washington.edu › dbpeds › Goodenough D.

Goodnow, J. (1977). Children drawing. Cambridge, MA : Harvard University Press. Gredler, M. E. (1997). Learning and instruction: Theory into practice. Upper Saddle River, NJ: Prentice-Hall.

John-Steiner, V. (1997). Notebooks of the mind: Explorations of thinking. Oxford: Oxford University Press.

Katz, L. G. & Chard, S. C. (1989). Engaging children's minds: The project approach. Norwood, N. J.: Ablex.

Kentridge, W., (n.d.), Retrieved 7th February, 2021 https://en.wikipedia.org/wiki/William_Kentridge

Kindler, A. M. (Ed.) (1997). Child development in art. Reston, Virginia: National Art Foundation.

Kindler, A. M. & Darras, B. (1997). A map of artistic development. In A. M. Kindler, (Ed.). (1997) Child Development in Art. Reston, Virginia: National Art Foundation.

Lauquet, G. H. (1927). Le dessin enfantin. Paris: Alcan.

Leont'ev, A. (1977/78). Activity, consciousness, and personality. Englewood Cliffs, NJ: Prentice-Hall.

Lindsay, G., 2021. Visual arts pedagogy in early childhood contexts: The baggage of self-efficacy beliefs, pedagogical knowledge and limited pre-service training. Volume 46, Issue 1, https://doi.org/10.1177/1836939120979061

Lindsay, G., 2017. Let's address low visual arts self efficacy. Australian Teacher Magazine, 221.

Malaguzzi, L., (1993) For an education built on trusting relationships. Young Children, 49(1), 9-12,

Google Scholar

Mau, B., 1998. Incomplete Manifesto for Growth, retrieved 7th February, 2021. https://www.google.com/

Moll, L. (1990). Vygotsky and education. New York: Cambridge University Press.

Newton, C. & Kantner, L. (1997). Cross-cultural research in aesthetic development:

A review. A. M. Kindler, Ed. (1997). Child Development in Art. Res- ton, Virginia: National Art Foundation.

Parson, M. (1998). Book review. Studies in art education: A journal of issues and research. 40(1) 80-91.

Print of thistle. Retrieved 7th February 2021. http://www.darvillsrareprints.com/images/images/Sowerby/11/Scotch-Thistle.jpg

Piaget, J. & Inhelder, B. (1969). The child's conception of space. London: Routledge and Kegan Paul.

Pollard, A., (Ed) (2015) Readings for reflective teaching. Bloomsbury, London.

Rinaldi, Carla., (2001) The pedagogy of listening: the listening perspective from Reggio. shinebright.org.au

Rogoff, B. (1990). Apprenticeship in thinking: Cognitive development in social context. New York: Oxford University Press.

Ruby, J. (2006) The last 20 years of visual anthropology–a critical review. Visual Studies, volume 20

Salome, R. A. & Reeves, D. (1972). Two pilot investigations of perceptual training of four and five year old kindergarten children. Studies in Art Education. 13, 2, 3-10

Smith, N. (1983). Drawing conclusions: Do children draw from observation? Art Education. 36 (5), 22-26.

Tharp, R. G. & Gallimore, R. (1988). Rousing minds to life: Teaching, learning and schooling in social context. Cambridge: Cambridge University Press.

Vecchi, V., (2010) Art and Creativity in Reggio Emilia: Exploring the Role and Potential of Ateliers in Early Childhood Education. Routledge.

Vygotsky, L, S. (1933) Play and its role in the Mental Development of the Child. Journal of Russian & East European Psychology https://www.marxists.org/archive/vygotsky/works/1933/play.htm

Vygotsky, L. S. (1962). Thought and language. Cambridge, Massachusetts: The M.I.T. Press

Vygotsky, L. S. (1978). Mind in society. Cambridge, Massachusetts: Harvard University Press.

Vygotsky, L. S. (1986). Thought and language. Cambridge, Massachusetts: The M.I.T. Press

Vygotsky, L. S. (1987). The collected works of L. S. Vygotsky (N. Minik, Trans. Vol. 1). New York: Plenum.

Vygotsky, L. S. (1997). Educational psychology. (R. Silverman, trans.). Boca Raton, FL: St. Lucie.

Vygotsky, L., (2004) Imagination and Creativity in Childhood. Journal of Russian & East European Psychology. Vol 42. Issue 1.

Wales, R. (1991). Children's pictures. In R. Grieve, (Ed.). Understanding children: Essays in honor of Margaret Donaldson. Oxford: Basil Blackwell, Inc.

Wertsch, J. (1985). Vygotsky and the social formation of mind. Cambridge, MA: Harvard University Press.

Wertsch, J. (2000). Vygotsky's two minds on the nature of meaning. In, Lee, C. D. & Smagorinsky, P. (Eds.). (2000). Vygotskian Perspectives on Literary Research: Constructing Meaning through Collaborative Inquiry. Cambridge University Press.

Wheeler, G. (2000). Learning in context [videorecording] : Probing the theories of Piaget and Vygotsky / the Open University. Princeton, NJ : Films for the Humanities & Sciences

Wilson, B. (1997) Types of Child Art and Alternative Developmental Accounts: Interpreting the Interpreters. Scholar.

Wilson, M. & Wilson, B. (1982). Teaching children to draw: a guide for teachers and parents. NJ: Prentice-Hall Inc.

Wink, J. & Putney, L. (2002). A vision of Vygotsky. Boston: Allyn and Bacon.

Wood, D., Bruner, J. & Ross, S. (1976). The role of tutoring in problem solving. Journal of Child Psychology and Psychiatry, 17,89-100

Zebroski, J. T. (1994). Thinking through theory: Vygotskian perspectives on teaching of writing. Portsmouth, NH: Boynton/Cook

If you have enjoyed this book you might be interested in the companion book *Authentic Art with Children*

Authentic Art with Children

Second Edition

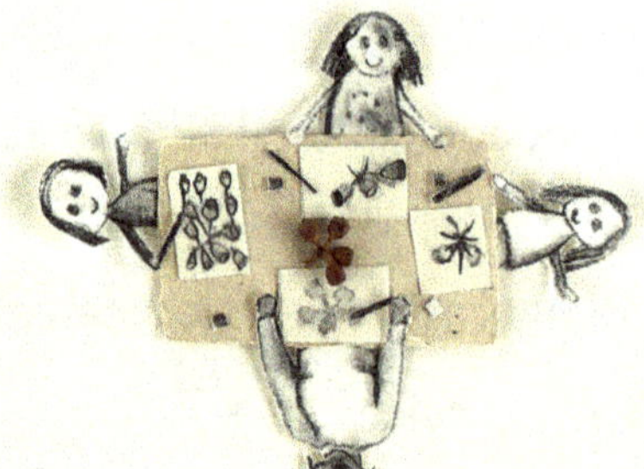

Dr. Margaret Brooks

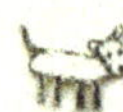